jamien.com
. . . .

The proceeds of this book will be used
to help fund an arts education enrichment
program for Maine island children as a
collaboration between the Island Institute and
the Farnsworth Art Museum, where a new wing
has been named in memory of Jamien E. Morehouse.

Jamien and her four boys, Tim, Sam and the twins, Micah and James at Hurricane Island, Penobscot Bay, Maine, in 1988 a few months before she was diagnosed with breast cancer.

jamien.com

Celebrating Her Journey

JAMIEN E. MOREHOUSE

FEBRUARY 4, 1951 - MAY 3, 1999

*Edited by Philip Conkling
and Cynthia Bourgeault*

CUSTOM DESIGNED flags, banners, pennants, vexilla, semaphors, jacks, standards, streamers, drapeaux, oriflamb, ensigns, labara, gonfalons, burgees, bunting, pavillons

FOR celebrations, weddings, long lost friends, tree houses, birthdays, blank walls, favorite aunts, new babies, sports events, bountiful gardens, successful businesses, new homes & grey days

The flags and banners throughout this book are representative of the works of art created at Liberty Banners Co. started by Jamien Morehouse in 1975. The fish, hats, teapots, angels, buddhas, and other art displayed in the pages of this book have been selected from the work and collections of Jamien Morehouse. The cover photograph was contributed by Earl Stevens who remembered the day he took it more than twenty years ago and his subject in the barn window. He named his first child after Jamien.

Copyright © 2000 by Philip Conkling, Island Institute
ISBN 0-942719-26-3

Front Cover Photo by Earl Stevens
Back Cover Photo by Peter Ralston
Book design by Edith Allard
Production by Paige Parker
Printing by J.S. McCarthy
Cover Printing by John P. Pow

Contents

Her Life	viii
Preface	xii
Introduction	xiv
Jamien.com Home Page	xvi
Casting the Net	1
Networking with Tea	17
Networks of the Heart	31
Moving from Strength to Strength	121
In Memoriam	157
Remembering to Breathe	181
Afterwords	237

I live with cancer. I know there is an otherwise.
--Jamien Morehouse, 48, Artist, Rockport, Maine
Submitted to *America's Favorite Poems*--The Favorite Poem Project Anthology,
"Otherwise" copyright 1996 by the Estate of Jane Kenyon.
Reproduced with permission of Graywolf Press, Saint Paul, Minnesota.

Otherwise
by Jane Kenyon

I got out of bed
on two strong legs.
It might have been
otherwise. I ate
cereal, sweet
milk, ripe, flawless
peach. It might
have been otherwise.
I took the dog uphill
to the birch wood.
All morning I did
the work I love.

At noon I lay down
with my mate. It might
have been otherwise.
We ate dinner together
at a table with silver
candlesticks. It might
have been otherwise.
I slept in a bed
in a room with paintings
on the walls, and
planned another day
just like this day.
But one day, I know,
it will be otherwise.

Jamien March 1, 1999

Her Life
May 6, 1999

JAMIEN MOREHOUSE, 48, wife of Philip W. Conkling and mother of Tim, Sam, Micah, and James, died at home on May 3, 1999, in Rockport, Maine. She was born in Lexington, Massachusetts, on February 4, 1951, the daughter of Richard and Elise V. Morehouse.

Jamien graduated from Lexington High School in 1969 and Middlebury College in 1973. Following college, she journeyed to Warsaw, Poland, to teach school. It was the beginning of a deep interest in travel, as well as a love of education. Upon her return to the States, she again took a teaching position, this time on the island of North Haven, Maine.

Jamien served as the director of the Children's Resource Center in Portland, Maine, and the Maine Teacher's Center in Rockport, Maine. Her advocacy of the environment -always a priority-became more focused when she took a position in the Environmental Education Department of the Office of Energy Resources in Augusta, Maine. Later, Jamien researched and wrote a curriculum for the Maine Audubon Society.

She met Philip Conkling while attending an environmental conference in Damariscotta, Maine. They were married in October of 1980, and moved to Rockport in 1984. Their first child, Tim, was born in 1982. Sam was born in 1984 and twin boys, Micah and James, followed in May of 1988. As the mother of four boys, Jamien was unequaled, pouring her love, energy, and creativity into motherhood the way hot tea flows into a china cup.
She was active as a volunteer in their classrooms, organizing poster contests, teaching units on art and conservation, and assisting whenever possible.
 She loved Peopleplace, a cooperative preschool in Camden, and continued to encourage and support the school's activities long after her own children had outgrown it.

Her love of the land, concern for the environment, and belief in our connection to the earth led her in 1989 to propose a newspaper column for *The Camden Herald* dealing with the then novel concept of recycling. She wrote

"Waste Watch" until May of 1993. Years later she was still receiving updates and information from those who shared her views and concerns.

Jamien's creativity knew no bounds. She was a gifted writer, a *cordon bleu* chef, and the force behind two successful businesses. For two decades she created custom flags and banners through her company, Liberty Banners, and in the 1990s she began experimenting with millinery, creating the Flea Circus Hat Company. Her passion for hats and for helping her community led her in 1998 to help organize the Mad Hatter's Extravaganza, a fundraising weekend to benefit New Hope for Women, a Rockland, Maine, organization aiding battered women. In spring of 1999, she once again donned a striking hat as the event grew in size and participation.

In 1998, Jamien and her sons Micah and Jamie designed a four-leaf clover-style pretzel that won them a trip to Altoona, Pennsylvania, as honored guests of the Benzel Pretzel Factory. The trip with the boys, in December 1998, was an experience she treasured. As was typical with any place Jamien visited, the people of Altoona were touched by her caring spirit and her deliberate approach to life.

Jamien believed strongly in community, and strove to find similarities-rather than differences-between cultures. "No matter where I travel, whether it's Siberia or Altoona, people have the same concerns," she mused. "We're really all the same, no matter where we live." She loved the rugged community of Vinalhaven, Maine. From toddlerhood on, Jamien spent every summer in a rambling house on Lane's Island amidst family and friends. "Vinalhaven is a very important part of my life," she said. She admired the people who called the island home, and knew it to be a place of healing, tranquility, and beauty.

Jamien was a member of the First Unitarian Universalist Church, in Rockland, Maine, and a tireless volunteer for many events and organizations, including Cash for Clothes, Outward Bound, and the Island Institute. She believed strongly in the power of women and in the "remarkable insight which seems to be particular to women." In 1986, she began inviting friends to share a cup of tea on the first day of spring and contemplate peace, justice, and the environment. "By drinking tea together," she wrote, "I believe we may, indeed, solve some of the greatest problems in the world."

Complementing her global concerns was Jamien's love of her home and family. She took the time to pen thoughtful notes, care for pets, fluff pillows, and snip unruly geraniums. She appreciated a glass of good wine as well as a pungent cup of cider. She could bluff in poker with a straight face, find a treasure amidst a pile of trash, and laugh so that her entire body shook with mirth. But what struck all who knew her, no matter how well, was her unique ability to listen, truly listen. It was a gift that she cultivated by focusing intently on those people and things she loved and on those who needed her love. She called it living deliberately.

"There are two ways to live your life," said Albert Einstein. "One is as though nothing is a miracle. The other is as though everything is a miracle." Jamien Morehouse's miraculous life touched all who knew her, and through the power of technology, many, many more who did not. She is remembered in a remarkable Web site where friends and family (and even strangers) have shared thoughts on her life and passage, at www.jamien.com.

Jamien is survived by her husband, Philip Conkling; her sons, Tim, Sam, Micah, and Jamie Conkling; her parents, Dick and Lee Morehouse; her brother, Bruce Morehouse; and her nephew, Tucker Morehouse. She was predeceased by her sister, Marcy Morehouse.

Services will be at the Rockport Opera House on Saturday, May 15 at 10:30 a.m., followed by a reception at Rockport Marine. At Jamien's request, you are invited to wear an interesting hat.

"The land means so much to me," Jamien often said. Keeping this in mind, friends who wish may make donations in her memory to the :

Vinalhaven Land Trust		Friends of Rockport Harbor
P. O. Box 268	or	P.O. Box 10
Vinalhaven, ME 04863		Rockport, ME 04856.

Written by Vicki Doudera, neighbor and friend, May 6, 1999

Preface

WHAT YOU ARE ABOUT TO READ is actually two stories rolled into one. The first is a profound and lasting tribute to Jamien Morehouse-wife, mother, artist, idealist, and passionate community-builder-whose richly purposeful life was cut short by breast cancer at the age of forty-eight. Through the shimmering words of tribute in these pages, reflecting like diamonds the light sparkling off the facets, we see and celebrate in Jamien's short life those virtues we all know in our hearts are the real ones--friendship, faithfulness, compassion, caring--but that too often get short shrift until it's tragically too late.

Perhaps the more extraordinary story, however, is the one below the surface waters, carved and chiseled in time. It is the story of a dramatic, almost alchemical fusion of hearts and minds that occurred in the last weeks before Jamien's death, on May 3, 1999, through the most unlikely medium of the Internet. In late March, watching the sand swiftly slipping through the hourglass of Jamien's waning life, and recognizing the need for closure among her many friends far flung and close by--and the impossibility of providing for it personally--her husband, Philip Conkling, founding director of the Island Institute; their oldest son, Tim, sixteen; and Jamien's brother, Bruce Morehouse, put up a Web site, **jamien.com**, to create "in this most impersonal of spaces" a place to do what could not be done in any other way.

The results were electric. From all corners of the world, as close as the next-door neighbors and as far aware as Ireland and Africa, readers logged on and comments poured in--600 postings comprising some 400 raw pages of tributes, memories, poetry, spiritual counsel, dreams and longing, and deepest fears confessed. As of the date of the memorial service, the site had received 175,000 "hits" from an estimated 17,000 visitors. As the pieces slowly stitched themselves together, what took shape, as one correspondent put it, was "a giant teach-in consciousness-raising" about presence in living and presence in dying.

Old friends, some from Jamien's earliest childhood days, found their way to her--and each other--once again. Some correspondents were close friends and neighbors, others total strangers moved by what they saw unfolding before their eyes. A six year old wishes Jamien "I hope you have a fun time up in heaven when you get there because I know you had a fun time here." Others, older and sadder, found themselves confessing burdens of grief long carried alone, or sharing moments of what can only be described as pure mystical presence. Still more homely and wondrous were descriptions of the moments of pure earthly presence: the sights and sounds of banners waving, the scent of pies, portraits of a Maine island, unforgettable vignettes of lugging children around or nursing babies on the ferry that were the tapestry of Jamien's life. And above all, a sense, as April gave slowly to May, and spring's coming and Jamien's waning life intertwined with escalating intensity, that the Web site had taken on a life of its own, had become a huge, pulsing network of the heart in which things perhaps too precious and intimate ever to be said in life, were actually, before the eyes, taking form.

"Is this the crowning piece in the portfolio of your loving?" writes one correspondent, an old chum from Hurricane Island days. And in a way she had named a profound truth. Jamien was perhaps always in life what is known as a "conceptual artist." Her highest artworks were not the banners, hats, pies, fish, and other artifacts she created, but a process in time: the process of raising four young sons to healthy, strong manhood; the process of weaving communities together; the artistry of noticing a new neighbor in distress and grief, of calling a young friend with newborn twins just as she is about to go out of her head with frustration and exhaustion. And so, in the last moments of her life, it was perhaps not only miraculous but inevitable that her great masterpiece should be this cyber-tapestry, existing no place but every place, woven out of scraps of memory and gratitude, stitching together what is forever imperishable in the human heart.

Cynthia Bourgeault
Managing Editor 1989-93
The Island Institute

Introduction

As a culture, we Americans share a well-deserved reputation for avoiding discussions of death and dying. We are energized by the infinite possibilities of life; we race headlong into our futures; we celebrate everything that is fresh and new.

When my wife, Jamien Morehouse, was first diagnosed with breast cancer in 1989 at age thirty-eight, we were like so many other people who receive devastatingly bad news. After we recovered from the awful shock of the words we had just heard, we quickly began to focus on a battle plan. I remember my words of promise to Jamien as if I had just spoken them, "Whatever it takes, Jamien, …whatever it takes."

We went in Boston to the Dana Farber Cancer Institute where surely the most renowned and best trained doctors in the medical community could help us defeat the cancer. They would help us because we were ready to do anything; they would help us because western technology was so ascendant that it was a matter of marshalling the talent, the resources, and the will to survive; and they would help us because our four boys, then six, four, and infant twins, desparately needed their mother. Our chances were good. Jamien was in excellent health; she had always been conscious of eating well; and we lived in a wonderful small town in mid-coast Maine where the air was clean and the water pure. Besides, there were plenty of success stories out there. We would be one of them.

During the next ten years before she was edged out at the finish line of her marathon race with cancer, we learned many powerful and ultimately transcendent lessons of life. But none was so important as the very first piece of wisdom we learned almost accidentally. In the first week following her diagnosis, I happened to meet with a friend of a friend about work when the subject of Jamien's diagnosis came up. My new acquaintance of less than a quarter of an hour immediately excused us and asked me to join him in his study. He sat behind his desk, a kindly eminence with snowy white hair. He surprised me by saying that he had been battling cancer for a dozen years; he had been the chief operating officer of Johnson and Johnson and had had access to all the best medical advice, all the therapies, treatments, and experimental drugs that western science had in its arsenal. But none of that, he said, was more important than what he was about to tell me. "You must," he said, "you absolutely must talk about Jamien's cancer with anyone and everyone. People will be looking to take their signals from you, and if you are reluctant to talk about cancer to others, the fear of it can eat you all alive." Or words to that effect. This advice was like a floating spar that drifts by after a shipwreck. We latched on to it because it was the only thing within reach that sounded like truth. And that simple dictum was ultimately a key to our lives for the next decade. It was the wisdom we carried with us as Jamien's time ran out.

Cancer is not easy to talk about; death is even harder. But that's not the point. None of us is really ready to be told our time is up. But pretending that if we avoid the subject, death won't still be out there waiting patiently or impatiently, just beyond our outstretched arms, is no way to live. It's like being afraid of the dark; it's a terribly heavy load to carry through life.

This book grew out of a Web site that was dedicated to the conviction that it was better to share the terrible pangs of loss in death honestly with friends and family rather than trying to contend with them stoically in private. Besides, the phone was ringing off the hook from loved ones who needed to know what was happening in the month and a half that Jamien lay dying. That in itself was an exhausting task and we needed an easier way to communicate.

The jamien.com Web site ultimately took on a life of its own rippling outward into the universe of distant relatives, old friends, lost lovers, even perfect strangers. Many people asked that we try to capture the essence of this site in book form. There were many reasons for wanting to do so; but none for me more profound than laying to rest forever the unspoken worry of our four sons that the memory of their mother might slowly fade over time. Not so; not ever.

Philip Conkling

jamien.com

Peter Ralston

○ *Memoriam*

○ *Images*

○ *Share your thoughts*

○ *Read others thoughts*

○ *Get an update*

○ *Tea*

○ *Email to Philip*

*In this most impersonal of spaces, perhaps we can meet
where otherwise we might not have been able to
and to communicate as perhaps we need to*

www. jamien.com

March 16, 1999

    As the sands run through the exquisite hourglass of her life, Jamien sends her love out to you in some small measure of return on the immense outpouring of heartfelt joy and care she has received from so many in recent months and weeks.

    Because her energy is preciously finite and she tires easily, it is not possible to see as many of you as she would wish in a different world, in a different time. Even though the computer medium is strange and new to her, she reaches out to you and asks you to hold her in your thoughts as she holds you in hers.

    Your messages and reminiscences posted on her new Web site will help speed her on her way as surely as the wings of angels have lightened her journey. The boys will download your e-notes and prayers to read them to Jamien and we'll keep the Web page updated.

    Many thanks,
    Philip, Tim, Sam, Micah, and Jamie Conkling

Casting the Net

What does the world look like when blind? What will I see without you? I can't imagine the world without you. You have always been there for me, for everyone it seems.

Bruce Morehouse, April 4, 1999

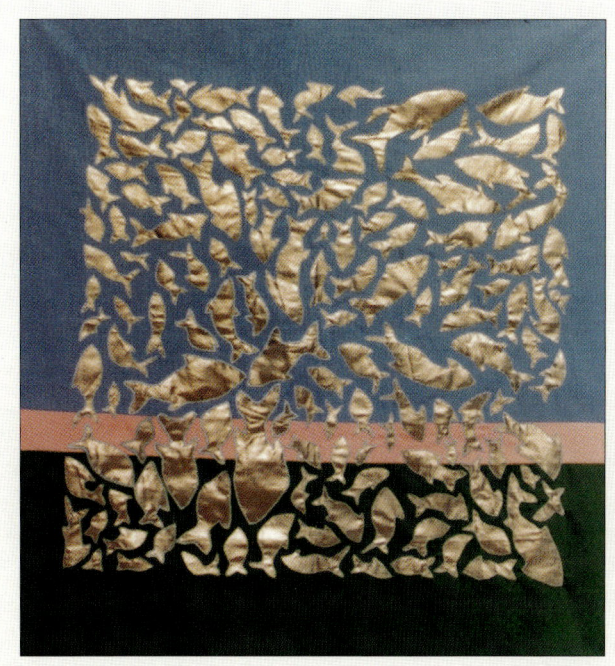

Bait Box 1979

Jamien's Welcome banner that hangs at Rockaway, Lane's Island

March 30
• • • •

Last week shortly after dark, Jamien heard voices outside her downstairs room and asked me to see who was there. I opened the front door and looked down the street. All I could see was a small river of flickering candles as a group of more than a hundred neighbors and friends rounded into view. They were mothers and fathers, grandparents, children, old and young. They stood in rows in front of the house and began softly singing Jamien's favorite songs. The boys, Tim, Sam, Micah and Jamie, gathered on the front steps and in the living room, tears streaming down their cheeks. The singing went on for a long while in the gathering darkness of night. Jamien stood at the door and leaned against the jamb, framed in the rose colored doorway of 11 Maple Street to thank everyone.

At the end of the songfest, many left their candles burning in the door yard before melting away into the night. The next morning, I got up early to run, and found amid the charred marks in the grass at the edge of the street, a pair of candles still burning as the sun struggled to the rim of the horizon. A pair of small miracles.

Philip

The letters that follow are selected from the many hundreds that were posted on the Jamien.com Web site.

Jamien, Middlebury College ca. 1971

Dearest Jamien,

I'm not at all sure that I can convey to you what you have come to mean to me. I first heard of you back when you wrote the "Waste Watch" column in *The Camden Herald*. I enjoyed each article and cut a few out to save (something I don't do very often). A few years later, you facilitated a recycling box project for an after-school enrichment that our oldest son, Lee, took. He enjoyed it and we still use that box to recycle everything that we can. Over the years, I heard your name from one person or another, and I was looking forward to meeting you at last.

What I discovered when that opportunity came was that you are one of those rare individuals who glow with an inner light that draws people to you. You radiate love and generosity to all whom you meet. You are a person who listens carefully to those around you, making each of us feel special and respected. You do it so effortlessly that I know it comes from your heart. There really is no good way to describe the impact you have had on those whose lives you have touched. I hear SO many people, who perhaps have not told you in person, speak of you with such high regard and respect and so much concern for your well-being. This community has taken you as much into our hearts as you have taken us into yours. I feel blessed for the times that we have spent together, although it was not that often--or maybe I might say not often enough! I know, for myself, you will always hold a very special place in my heart--for your beauty of spirit, your generous heart, your sense of adventure, your laughter, and your courage.

May you always walk in beauty, my friend.

Love,

Jan Warren <ragged1@mint.net>
Camden, ME USA - Friday, April 02, 1999 at 14:52:51 (EST)

My Dear Jamien,

We don't really know each other; you kindly know my name enough to so pleasantly say hello when we meet, and I know of your courage and integrity throughout all you do.

When my father was passing I was the one to let him go. He knew each of his six adult children better than we might have guessed. And I knew that I had to give him permission to give up his fight at last. When most had left the room after that last sad meeting, I leaned over and whispered into his ear. Some guided imagery, but mostly permission. We were going to be all right. Really, that was his biggest concern.

You also will leave your family and friends in the best of hands. All you have done has led you here and though they stand on the edge of the abyss peering into the unfathomable darkness, they, and you, know that bridges will be built to guide them over.

The kids [are] in Philip's hands and Philip [is] in God's own loving hands as well as those of your legions of friends. And you will have the joy of watching them from your next journey: watching them grow, watching Philip grow, and each reveling in the innumerable gifts you have given them. You have done your job well. And now as we each have learned and received from you, let us have this opportunity to give back.

We all will be part of your family in our hearts and our actions. And proudly so.

Geoff Parker <islprd@midcoast.com>
Rockport, ME USA - Friday, April 02, 1999 at 15:24:12 (EST)

Dear Jamien,

When I asked you what I could do for you a few months ago, you said, "Pray." Every morning I begin my day in front of my meditation table. The candle is lit, the light flickers on the walls of my studio, and as I sit in silent prayer and meditation, the first sunlight of the morning begins to strike the very tops of the trees in the woods behind the barn. On this table I place special items--shells, stones, feathers, pictures of family, and small, special notes that contain the names of people I say a special prayer for. Your name has been on my meditation table for the past three months. I have been saying a daily prayer for you since we spoke. I want you to know, I will continue to hold this prayer for you: may you make this transition in peace and not suffer in pain. Thank-you for reaching out to me.

   Love, Lynn

Ivan & Lynn Stancioff <Stanivan@tidewater.net>
Lincolnville, ME USA - Saturday, April 03, 1999 at 06:01:36 (EST)

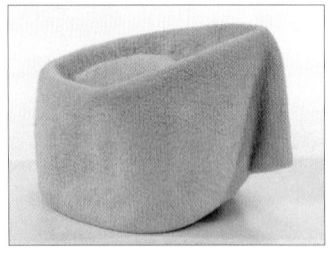

DEAR FRIEND JAMIEN,

   You have no idea how much it meant to me to arrive home on Wednesday and find a bag on my door handle with this fuzzy white thing in it. When I took it out and realized what it was I felt sad to realize the time had come for the hand-me-down of a prized hat from the collection of the millinery goddess. A hat I had all too selfishly coveted and nearly weaseled out of you. But it looked so good on you, as do most hats. It just has a certain air and flair about it from a bygone era. A certain attitude and personality. Proper in its simplicity. Regal in its minimalism. Best in off-white.

   The fact that you remembered and sent it along means a great deal to me. I want you to know I am honored and thrilled to have it!

   With gratitude and love to you, my dear, Amy

Amy Fischer <goldfish@midcoast.com>
Camden, ME USA - Saturday, April 03, 1999 at 14:12:27 (EST)

DEAR JAMIEN,

This is just silly…you have made me feel SANE! I had no idea how to raise a boy, and many laughed or shook their heads when my little one wanted to be as pretty as his older sister. Sometimes he showed up dressed in tutu and beads at Peopleplace, and I found such JOY and COMFORT in seeing that you had such a relaxed attitude about it all.

Hell, your kids had lady's hand bags as lunchboxes!

You made me feel that it was okay to just let kids explore and be themselves, and in due time they would figure things out. What funny and happy memories I have of those years.

Now he's building catapults and setting horrible traps all around the house… I can't imagine having four of them around. You are one heck of a mom!   AND I love you.

Kalla <hilltop@midcoast.com>
Camden, me USA - Saturday, April 03, 1999 at 15:04:11 (EST)

DEAR JAMIEN,

When I look at Sam, Tim, and the twins I see the love and care you have been able to put into raising them, living with the terrible thing you must live with. That itself is a HUGE inspiration, because it shows that anyone can do anything if they put their heart into it. I think it is unfortunate that it takes these extremes for some people to realize this, but if they do then you can rest easy knowing that you have made many people very, very happy.

Love, Ben Dorr *[Age fifteen]*

P.S. When your moment comes you will fly higher than the rest of us.

Benjamin Dorr <Benjamin_Dorr0@fivetowns.net>
Camden, ME USA - Saturday, April 03, 1999 at 16:24:26 (EST)

Jamien with Micah at Peopleplace,
a cooperative nursery school where Jamien worked and volunteered

7

DEAR JAMIE AND FAMILY,

    I was just walking down Main Street, Vinalhaven, thinking about Easter baskets, when I met Karen Jackson. She told me about this incredible Web site, and I thought, of course, how like Jamie to find a way for her friends to share their feelings. Jamie, you're always learning something new and eagerly sharing it with the rest of us. Those early morning qi gong sessions at the quarry were so extraordinary. My love to you all as you face this greatest of life's mysteries.

Elaine Crossman <tidewater@foxislands.net>
Vinalhaven, Me USA - Saturday, April 03, 1999 at 16:44:11 (EST)

DEAR JAMIEN AND PHILIP AND LEE AND DICK
[Lee and Dick Morehouse are Jamien's parents],

    How great to have this means of communicating....I have wanted to contact you, but hated the idea of that jangling phone. This comes to you ALL with my biggest hugs and most healing thoughts. I have been with you through the ups and downs of the last years, and I am moved and awed at how you have coped with such trials.

    Jamien, I think our most meaningful times, at least for me, were our hours together on the Dump Committee. We met in that filthy room (Barry's "office") in the shack next to the garbage pit. Every surface was covered with a greasy film, and we sat on salvaged treasures which had been spurned by the Swap Shop. We had an "air purifier," actually just the shell of one, but we loved twirling its dial when Sonny's cigarette smoke got thick.

    You would arrive with muffins for all of us, and a complete kindergarten for the twins. They would settle in on the floor (yuck!) on a quilt and play happily while we conducted the Dump's business. One day, when the giant trucks were rumbling by with excessive noise and vibration en route to the pit, one of the twins looked up from his crayons and asked "Are we almost at the ferry landing, Mommy?"

Time with you, Jamien, was always merry, and I loved the brief moments we shared over the years. I feel close to your family and hope these days will be peaceful, fulfilling, and full of the love that SO many feel for you all. My dearest love comes with this message.

Sonia

Sonia Spalding <budson@midcoast.com>
Camden, ME USA - Saturday, April 03, 1999 at 16:48:50 (EST)

Dear Jamien,

I remember the day of your wedding. I was waiting for my daughter to be born and the doctor thought it best that I not take the ferry. It was such a gray, dreary October day but I kept looking out over the water thinking of you. I remember looking up just as the ceremony must have been starting and somehow the sky cleared and the sun came out. I thought, How magical! How Jamie! You are so dear to my heart.

Love, Sara

sara <sarag@sad50.k12.me>
waldoboro, me USA - Saturday, April 03, 1999 at 16:58:02 (EST)

Dear Jamien,

Years ago when Elaine received her first invitation to share a worldwide spot of tea at your urging, I was first moved by your capacity for inspiration. Since then I've had occasion time and again for taking encouragement from your great strength and vision and from your gift of staggering resolve. You've been a beacon to more of us than you know and You Can't Be A Beacon If

Your Light Don't Shine.

I'll anticipate my own transition much more sweetly knowing that you will have been there a while challenging who ever is in charge, bucking the odds, and stirring things up.

Phil Crossman <tidewater@foxislands.net>
Vinalhaven, Me USA - Saturday, April 03, 1999 at 18:52:40 (EST)

Jamien, age six, Moon Hill

DEAREST JAMIE,

I wish I could say I remember when we first met what feels like half a century ago and very nearly is. You were lost for me in that swarm of tiny beings who crawled over the summit of Moon Hill in the 1950s, blending in with all those Fletchers, Thompsons, and Harkness girls.

It wasn't until we grew bigger, riding bikes, scabbing knees, spinning bottles, that I began to sense what was special about you. How I envied you your handsome parents, your designer home, your seemingly effortless creativity. Was it my imagination, or did our mothers harbor fantasies that we would someday end up together?

It was impossible, of course. We were all too much like brothers and sisters, the Moon Hill Diaspora, set off to the four corners of New England for college, careers, and children. When we reunited haphazardly in Lexington or Vinalhaven, though, we still seemed connected, or at least on parallel tracks. Your Philip. Our writing. Everybody's twins. *[Philip Elmer-DeWitt and his wife, Mary, had twins shortly after Jamien and Philip Conkling.]*

I can't be the only one who has had difficulty these past few years reconciling the tumor that was growing inside you with this ruddy-faced woman who seemed to be glowing with health and aliveness. Now they tell me you are dying. How I wish there were something I could do to ease your pain or your family's anguish. I don't pretend to know where you are going. I like to think you are returning somewhere you love, laughing and crying and blending in with all those who went before you.

Philip Elmer-DeWitt <ped@well.com>
Brooklyn, NY - Sunday, April 04, 1999 at 12:30:37 (EDT)

Middlebury College Twenty-fifth Reunion Flag

DEAR JAMES,

What a cold, dark Easter morning it was here! Thankfully the sunrise service was held inside the warm church. The sun's broken out now, though, and it's warming the day, as I hope it is for you all. Such warmth you must be receiving from all these messages!! It's like birthday morning every day as you relish your "cards" from friends. And don't you deserve it! Payback time for all the gifts you've shared with us.

I'm remembering again your birthday "happening" in college when we all piled onto the bed you'd dragged over to Johnson. What hilarity and fun stuff you created! You have the natural spirit to be the life of the party, James, and I'm picturing us all now, gathered at your bed in the dining room at 11 Maple, sharing time, stories, laughs, and love. We're all so much happier for your creativity and fun!!

My love to you, with prayers for peace, Lindy-o

Lindy O. Sargent <libnpc@pop.k12.vt.us>
Orleans, VT USA - Sunday, April 04, 1999 at 15:37:48 (EDT)

DEAR JAMIEN, PHILIP, AND FAMILY,

I have thought about you all today and said a special prayer for you in church this morning. What tremendous courage you have shown me, Jamien, throughout the years. You continue to inspire me.

We loved being part of the songfest in your honor and what a special gift I

11

Stars Above, Stars Below 1978

could share with my children, who really do not understand all this sadness. Thank you for reaching out yet again. We loved the songs that were chosen and I understand they were your favorites.

The wind is howling outside and I look out to the islands and think what a big part of them you are. Thank you for touching me in so many ways.

Much love, Caroline

Caroline Morong <beanie@midcoast.com>
Camden, MME USA - Sunday, April 04, 1999 at 18:57:06 (EDT)

Dearest Jamien,

On this Easter Sunday, my son, Ian, and I were having a discussion about church and prayer, which he has felt little need to incorporate in his life thus far. He asked me, "Well, what would I pray for?" And of course, my thoughts turned to you and your family. You have been part of my prayers for a long time, though we seldom have crossed paths in recent years. Your creativity and strength, your clear vision of the things of real value in life, have been a wonder and beauty to me. You and your family continue to be in my thoughts and prayers.

My love is with you, Kathleen

Kathleen Oliver <olivers@mint.net>
Lincolnville, ME USA - Sunday, April 04, 1999 at 20:21:46 (EDT)

For a number of years I worked daily restoring an old house on Vinalhaven. To my surprise and disappointment, it was a strangely anonymous affair. It seemed to me that all who lived, labored, loved, and died in this place were not as "present" as I expected them to be. I searched for signs, for clues to the details and meaning of their lives, and found precious few. I longed to know the people whose work I was undoing, and then doing again. I was saddened by these quiet timbers and stones.

As I contemplate what I know of you, Jamie, I am struck by how yours has not been a silent life. It sounds, it rings, it echoes. Your presence in the lives of others, as long as I have known you, is tangible and profound. Your life proclaims: I am here.

With love, Gigi and Karol

Gigi Baas <folkwear@midcoast.com>
Vinalhaven, ME USA - Sunday, April 04, 1999 at 20:31:57 (EDT)

DEAR JAMIE ET AL.,

As I sat in church this morning, I thought of all of the people who had come before me who had some influence on the person I am today. Living in one place for many generations certainly gives families roots, but no matter where we live, we are influenced in some part by those who came before us.

We live on in all of those whose lives we have touched. It is true that no man is an island and some of us touch more souls than others. This Web site is proof of your sphere of influence.

Donna Miller Damon <Donna_Damon@onf.com>
Chebeague Island, ME USA - Sunday, April 04, 1999 at 21:03:33 (EDT)

What does the world look like when one is blind? What will I see without you? You who took me fishing at Spy Pond (and you picked up Pip on the way back, wondering what Mom would say) and I caught that little perch you drew. (Did you know I ended up living on Spy Pond and still have that drawing?) Our stowing away on trains in Lapland, our forays into abandoned buildings, skinny-dipping, kite flying, pyrotechnics, parties, clothes, masonite fish with legs, peanut chocolate clusters, long talks and tears.

Changes, I don't want changes, I want it to go on as it was. My keys are slippery and my vision blurred. I can't imagine the world without you. You have always been there for me, for everyone it seems. You still will be, I know, in different ways I cannot imagine. It will be altogether different. You have attained that immortality through us all. Much is dormant, to awaken at the right time, perhaps generations later. I cannot imagine life without you. I revel in the thought of what you have created and set in motion in this lifetime. I have felt and will feel differently because of you. I wish we could dance naked on the earth and go swimming under the stars and howl at the moon, such is the lightness I feel when I think of you.

Know that you have done enough. Peace be with you.

Bub <baggedmail@acadia.net>
Belfast, ME - Sunday, April 04, 1999 at 21:54:42 (EDT)

["Bub" is Bruce Morehouse, Jamien's brother.]

DEAREST JAMIEN,

I don't know if it's because we are both mothers of twins and have a common bond of Vinalhaven, or that we both love to create fun and whimsical things, but I have always felt an incredible respect for you and a deep regret that we have never had the chance to truly get to know one another.

I will never forget the time I called you about an upcoming show and you were laboriously boiling (and being grossed out at the same time) a whole fish with the eyeballs bulging out of their sockets. That was a very animated conversation!

Oh yes, those fish…fish with legs, fish without legs. My Jamien fish has been hanging in the kitchen since 1993. All your work, an inspiration to me. I always dreamed that, like you, I, someday too, would have my motel in the woods in which to create and meditate.

Jamien, you are a true inspiration to all of us and I send this Easter greeting to you and your family with love, blessings, and a tremendous gratitude for knowing you--you with a heart as big as the world.

Diana Kerr
Trevett, Me USA - Sunday, April 04, 1999 at 22:28:20 (EDT)

DEAR JAMIEN,

Thought you'd like to know that every Sunday now, including yesterday, Easter, I'm wearing the stole you made me. It is beautiful--marvelous colors and expert quilting--a perfect reflection of your beauty (inner and outer), your creativity, your blessedness--all of which you have shared freely with so many of us over the years. What a God-given treasure you were for all of us!

Just know how much you mean to all of us, how much you add to our lives, how much we love you, and how we're thinking of you and praying right beside you. Please know that you are in the prayers and thoughts of our little church down here in Stoughton. Blessed be, dear soul.

Jeff Symynkywicz and Elizabeth and Sarah and Noah and Micah

Jeff Symynkywicz <revjeff@worldnet.att.net>
Stoughton, MA USA - Monday, April 05, 1999 at 09:21:16 (EDT)
[Jeff is the former minister of the Unitarian-Universalist church in Rockland, where he was presiding when Jamien first discovered her breast cancer.]

JAMIE:

I am so grateful to have this way of communicating with you. I think of you so often, and now I can "send" these thoughts to you just as fast as thinking them. Whoever came up with this idea was truly inspired.

My first thought after reading all of these heartfelt messages was, what a gift cancer can be--if it gives us the chance, a golden chance, to say goodbye and reconnect while there is time. I realized this after my [own] diagnosis, and this awareness gave me a reason to accept cancer in a positive way. The things I have read from your friends have allowed me to get to know you even better and have re-affirmed what I already had guessed: You are an amazing woman!!!!!!

You are a heroine to look up to. I want to have your courage when my time comes, but I'll look forward to seeing you then...

Love, Allison

Allison Cooke Brown <bpb@ceimaine.org>
Yarmouth, ME USA - Sunday, April 04, 1999 at 23:26:54 (EDT)

Networking with Tea

. . . .

My memory of you shines like your smile--about the most beautiful smile I've ever seen--like your joyful compassionate wit. Jamie, your spirit flows among us.

Ashley Caldwell, April 5, 1999

Watercolor by Carolyn Brady

Tea Ceremonies

March 16, 1999

Dear Friends, well met and yet to be met,

   Back in 1986, Jamie Morehouse started a wonderful tradition of sharing a cup of tea with her women friends, wherever they were in the world, once a year on a specified day. This humble gathering has been such a simple yet warm celebration of the roles, the spirit, the energies, the ideas, the visions, the strengths and weaknesses, the tasks, the camaraderie…all the various threads that define and intertwine us all. Much has taken place in the years between 1986 and 1999. Over these years the threads have been woven into a different fabric of life for each and every one of us. Jamie's own tapestry is a picture of courage and strength. Its warp is strung with creativity, purpose, and determination; its weft made of fathomless kindness, love, and generosity. It is beautiful and strong.

   For Jamie, the weaving of her physical life is nearly complete. Beyond desperately wishing that I could unravel the cursed disease that has gripped her for so long or, at the very least, wishing that I could erase her pain, my most acute frustration has been to be physically far away from her. I imagine the same may be true for many of you.

   I think of sharing a cup of tea all together as we have done in the past as one small way of bridging that gap and celebrating Jamie's special tapestry. And so, I would like to propose that we all share a cup with Jamie on April 5, 1999, at 4:00 p.m. EDT (when we can enjoy the wonderful sense of extra daylight granted by turning the clocks ahead). Let us enjoy the company and the warmth and peace that come from togetherness. Let's share the love that makes a quilt out of all our pieces. As Jamien wrote many years ago, "It will be a powerful gathering on a most gentle level." Please join us.

   With love, Wendy Elcome Harris *[Jamien's first cousin]*

The Original (1986) Tea Ceremony Invitation

Rockport, Maine
March 1986

DEAR FRIENDS,

I've collected a number of turning-point experiences these months: becoming thirty-five, sharing genuine grief with friends, growing children--enough to make me realize again that it's time to reevaluate those things that comprise my life. The old question of how am I using my energies--as a woman, mother, wife, daughter, sister, friend--in the balance of things that really matter.

Following a recent Sally Rogers concert in Portland, some simple things came clear again. (Why do we need reminding of simple things?) The basic messages were of love and peaceful legacies for our children. Yes, how simple. Harmony of song and heart, it is delicate and womanly…and fiercely strong.

Another thing I was reminded of this weekend, spent with my dear friend June, also a mother, wife, daughter, sister, was how delightful it is to spend time over a cup of tea with people you love. Don't you imagine a remarkable number of women have spent remarkable hours drinking tea together? Our mothers, grandmothers, and great-grandmothers? And what about the things they discussed? Imagine bottling that sense of camaraderie, unity, and woman-politicking for world-wide distribution. It's a lovely thought.

So I invite you to join me and many friends for tea. There's enough here to brew two cups: one for you and one for a friend. Thursday, March 20, is the first day of spring. Let's drink together on that day at

4:00 (my mother calls that "having foursies") Eastern Standard Time: a moment to share with a friend, many friends, all over the country, to commit ourselves to a springtime of rejuvenation and good humor, and a lifetime of peace, for the sake of our great-granddaughters, that they may take tea together as well.

Do enjoy it, and if you're so inclined, write down a few thoughts about this moment. My business partner, Carol, has suggested that we record and collect all our reflections; I'll type them up and mail them to any who respond.

I love you, Jamien

P.S. I gave my sons a tea set for Valentine's Day this year; they'll join us for tea. Perhaps your children would like to join us as well.

1990 Tea Ceremony Invitation

Rockport, Maine
March 1990

DEAR FRIEND,

I am sending you this invitation knowing that you share my feelings about living deliberately. I also know you probably love drinking tea with friends as much as I. (I'll not be sending tea to you, by the way, as I am hoping thousands of us will be participating in this party.)

As you sip your tea, enjoying the warmth of both the tea and your friends, I hope you'll exchange some ideas about how we can be vehicles of justice for all people. What small (and not so small) deeds can we perform to promote peace throughout the world? How can our commitment to love in our homes spill over into our neighborhoods, our cities, our countries? How can our sense of beauty and care for our homes be reflected in the environment?

I like the words of Marian Wright Edelman and I pass them on to you as valuable tenets to consider while you drink your tea.

- Assign yourself. Don't wait for someone else to direct you; figure out what needs to be done and do it.
- Never work just for money or power. They won't save your soul or build a decent family or help you sleep at night.
- Take parenting and family life seriously and insist that those you work for and who represent you do.
- Be confident that you can make a difference. Continue to make small waves and you will erode the complacency of the unjust.
- Don't be afraid of hard work or teaching your children to work.
- Always remember that you are never alone.

Enjoy your tea and good company.

In peace, Jamien

P.S. If you'd like to share some thoughts about your tea party, please drop me a line. Jamien Morehouse, 11 Maple Street, Rockport, Maine 04856.

1993 Tea Ceremony Invitation

PLEASE JOIN US FOR TEA
4:00 P.M., MARCH 20, 1993

I believe some of the world's greatest problems have been solved by women sitting at kitchen tables drinking tea. I see children crawling beneath these tables, cookie crumbs on the floor, perhaps a washing machine thumping in the corner. I see women kneeling at tables in felt-covered yurts with sleeping babies slung over their shoulders. I see women in mud-floored huts conversing with a friend or two while simultaneously refereeing their children's play.

They are all drinking tea together and they are sharing what it means to keep homes, to be wives, to raise children, have dreams, and wonder about the future. They laugh together, comfort one another, and call upon the remarkable insight which seems to be particular to women.

In 1986 I sent packages of tea to 100 friends and suggested that they each invite a friend to join them over a cup of tea at 4:00 on March 20, the first day of spring. Over 200 of us had tea together that day, all over the globe, and together we shared those things so uniquely our own. One woman told me she drank her tea while dashing from her office to her child's daycare center. Another drank hers in the barn while tending her sheep. Another took hers to the home of an elderly neighbor. Many shared their thoughts with me via letter and I was reminded that the strength and love that come from the most simple, domestic deeds are not to be underestimated.

I suggest that on the first day of spring, March 20, 1993, we drink tea together again. It will be a powerful gathering on a most gentle level. It will be a time to reflect on what it means to be a woman in the 1990s and on where we will take our collective spirit into the next century. It will be a confirmation of that which we, as women, have always known--that the skills of keepers of homes and nurturers of children are the skills which will ultimately bring a sense of love and caring to the world. Women's priorities are global priorities. By drinking tea together, I believe we may, indeed, solve some of the greatest problems in the world.

Jamien Morehouse
W.A.N.D., Women's Action for New Directions, Winter 1992/93

JAMIE,

   I will look forward to stopping whatever needs doing in the Statehouse at 4:00 p.m. tomorrow to drink a cup of tea. I will think of you, your wonderful boys, and Philip. I will think of your great beauty and spirit and all we continue to learn from you. I will think of how much I laughed when you told the story of your dog visiting a psychic. I will think of all the pictures I have in my mind of you--on my island and yours, on Hurricane or the mainland, with babies, teenagers, or other women. I will pray for you, hold you in my heart, and ask those around me to do the same.

   I hope the spring sunlight is shining in on you.

   The kids and I send our love and thanks--Chellie

Chellie Pingree <pingree@midcoast.com>
North Haven, ME USA - Sunday, April 04, 1999 at 21:56:08 (EDT)

DEAREST JAMIEN,

   Tom and I have returned from celebrating his fiftieth and we thought of you often during our trip. Swimming through the fishes I remembered the forty individual, beautiful fishes you painted, cut out, and taped up all over my house while I was out, to surprise me on my fortith birthday. Every present you have ever given me still holds a special place in this house because they were all so unique and special. In addition to these physical reminders of your love and friendship, I am grateful for the sweet and the difficult times we have shared when the gift of friendship held together the crazy emotions of "growing-up." Remember the Easter we went canoeing in Newcastle?

   Thank you for the privilege of putting your name on the school emergency cards for all these years because you are someone my children have always loved and trusted, as have Tom and I.

We will join you for tea. May peace be with you and with your spirit.

With love, Mary

Mary Amory <amory@midcoast.com>
Camden, ME USA - Monday, April 05, 1999 at 08:27:28 (EDT)

Dear Jamie,

We just got home Saturday from Florida to find you online! I had been sending you thoughts of love all month without the benefit of cyberspace…now I have another way! Leave it to your guys to bring you into the computer era…they are such bright, shining lights.

We have been thinking of you all so often. While in Florida, I taught Emma "Tue, Tue Bahrima, Tue, Tue" and the thread of that melody wound through our days, reminding me of the time you taught it to us out at Rikki's, and we danced and sang in the late summer afternoon. Emma sings it in a high, flutey voice, but whenever I hear it, I think of proud, capable women with strong shoulders, big hips, and feet solidly on the ground, connected to the earth. It reminds me of you.

We all have threads like this, woven into memories of special moments. And I have so many pictures in my mind as well. One is from the tea you gave last summer on the porch at Rockaway. We are floating above the world in the fog and the soft, gentle beauty of the afternoon. There are flowers and delicate china; there are savory treats and delicious tea. There is the sound of poetry and laughter. Above all, there are friends, sharing and savoring the preciousness of the moment together that you have created and given to us as a gift. Thank you. I raise my cup of tea to you, Jamie, as we all share another cup together this beautiful April afternoon.

With much love, Alice

Alice Bissell <abissell@foxislands.net>
Vinalhaven, ME USA - Monday, April 05, 1999 at 09:50:22 (EDT)

Dear Jamien,

On Easter Sunday at the small church I attended in Lincolnville women wore hats decorated to celebrate the coming of spring. There were several brightly colored and exotic hats and I thought of you. I know each year you organized a terrific weekend where women exhibited and sold their cherished hats. I can't help but smile when I think of the joy it brought. You and your family are in my prayers in this season of renewed hope and new life. I will join you and the host of others for tea at 4:00 p.m.

    Annette

Annette Naegel <annette@mint.net>
Camden, ME USA - Monday, April 05, 1999 at 13:50:34 (EDT)

Jamie,

I just wanted to let you know that I think your tea time is a beautiful idea reflecting what a beautiful, strong person you are.

At seven o'clock my time, four o'clock your time, my friends and I will raise our cafeteria tea cups in hope for a healthy, sunny, blooming spring for you. You are truly a rock star, Jamie, and even out here in Oregon we observe it. Take care.

    Lots of love to you, Philip, and your wild boys, Cecily Pingree

cecily pingree <pingree@lclark.com>
Portland, OR USA - Monday, April 05, 1999 at 15:46:51 (EDT)
[Cecily Pingree, eithteen, daughter of Chellie Pingree -page 21-wrote from her college in Oregon.]

Dear, dear Jamie,

I think of you and your family often, especially so these last few months, and I cherish memories of times spent with all of you. I remember picnics at

Fish Offerings, 1981, a private commission, photographed while hanging outside 11 Maple Street, Rockport

Winter Harbor, dinners at Rockaway, Saturday mornings at the flea market, and several times that you and the boys helped bring the Whaler around or take it back at the end of our stay. One year, we stopped the boat for a memorable lunch drifting in Long Cove. You were wearing a great pair of sunglasses with orange (?) frames that looked like the '30s, and I asked you where you got them. I was mightily impressed when you said, "I got them at the dump!"

Jamie, you have found beauty in the commonplace and made the rest of us aware of the beauty surrounding us. Your smile, your upbeat spirit, and your strength and grit have inspired everyone whose life you've touched. I'm pleased that my daughters have such fond memories of you and your family, and I feel truly honored to have known you.

Much love, Geoff

Geoff Getman <gcgetman@yahoo.com>
Baltimore, MD USA - Monday, April 05, 1999 at 21:22:49 (EDT)

I'm getting to my cup of tea a little later in the day than I'd planned, but as I sip it I remember the day that I was sitting at home with our newborn twins, sleep-deprived, overwhelmed, teary, guilt-ridden (how could I possibly do this to our #1 daughter?, etc.) and you called, Jamie. We didn't know each other well at all, but I felt that we had an instant rapport that day, and since. I've loved knowing you and the times we've been able to really talk have been too few. I've so admired your energy and courage these past few years. If I was comfortable with the notion of God, I'd send my prayers and blessings. As it is, I'll just say goodbye, and hope that we meet again (who knows?).

Love, Mary

mary elmer-dewitt <medewitt@aol.com>
brooklyn, ny USA - Monday, April 05, 1999 at 21:23:43 (EDT)

Hey there Jamien,

    i must say that it is an honor to share your name. You have made me proud to have the name that most everyone mispronounces upon initial encounter (some of my favorites: hah-mien and jameen, among many others). you're a legend-- the impact you have had on others is easily discernable from these letters. i can only hope to have such an influence. your many admirable qualities are documented here, not just from good friends, but brief acquaintances, and it becomes obvious to me (and everyone for that matter) how much of an amazing person you are. i promise to try and do the name 'jamien' some justice, by always remembering the star i was named after.

    love to you, jamien

Jamien Shields <jv_shields@cc.colorado.edu>
Colorado Springs, CO USA - Monday, April 05, 1999 at 21:23:45 (EDT)

[Jamien Shields is a young woman from North Haven Island, Maine, whose mother knew Jamien as the kindergarten teacher on the island in 1977.]

Dear Jamie,

    It's nice having tea with you, Wild Berry ZINGER, with honey, like you. I've rung our big meditation bell and you've come in on the waves.

    It's easy to think of you, even though our last conversation on the front steps of Old Chapel [during reunion] was years ago…and our canoe trip was half a life ago. Our week on the river was one of the highlights of my life-- being with you and Sneak and Louise--a briefly self-contained quartet, loving the river and each other…makes me weep to remember the simple joy of it. THANK YOU.

    And, now your friend, Wendy, writes that your "weaving of physical life is nearly complete." I wish you 10,000 times the peace you have given others (+me). I pray that your passing is 10,000 times more glorious than our nights on the Penobscot.

My memory of you shines like your smile--about the most beautiful smile I've ever seen--and like your joyful, compassionate wit. Paddle on Jamie, for your spirit flows among us.

I love you, Jamie. Ashley

Ashley Cadwell <acadwell@stmichaelschool.org>
St. Louis, MO USA - Monday, April 05, 1999 at 21:40:59 (EDT)

DEAR JAMIE,

We want to thank you for the gift of words, insights, and memories that you gave to the Willauer family from the pulpit at Betty's memorial service less than three months ago. Both of us were so impressed by your beauty, composure, and crystal clear memories of Betty, which (thanks to you) have now become our memories. Your good humor about "the male maelstrom" that you and Betty lived among, made Charlie and me laugh out loud, as we live in our own "male maelstrom" among our three boys. Of all the tributes to Betty that day, yours is the one we will cherish forever.

Through Betty, of course, we have followed your battle with cancer over the years and your efforts have been greatly admired by the entire Willauer clan. We wish you peace.

Charlie & Gale Willauer <willauer@thecia.net>
Duxbury, MA USA - Monday, April 05, 1999 at 22:16:48 (EDT)

DEAREST JAMIE,

It's not lost on me that I'm writing this via Tim--to think that your son and I would wind up in the same business so many years later! When was it, 1977, when we met? I think that you were setting up the Children's Resource

Center in Westbrook, and I was a lowly assistant professor at UMPG. Twenty-one years ago? And then we moved to Santa Barbara.

When we got Wendy Harris's letter yesterday it was clear that if I am going to make contact with you again, now's the time. I can't exactly say why this news has affected me so. I am saddened and touched in a way I cannot fathom. Sheila tells me that it's simply because of who you are, Jamie. That even though our lives crossed for only brief moments, the light you shed on us will blaze forever.

I want to tell your boys and your husband that they are blessed by having you in their lives. I want to tell you that you have been in my heart since the day we met, and will continue to live there always. Sheila and I are not religious by any stretch, but we will both create the most positive energy for you in the days ahead. We will share a cup of tea together next week. Our love is with you. Godspeed, Jamie.

Love, Gordon and Sheila

Gordon and Sheila Morrell <gordon@yardi.com>
Santa Barbara, CA USA - Monday, April 05, 1999 at 23:16:34 (EDT)

DEAREST JAMIE,

I will never be able to forget tea today. I thought of the miracle of many, many other hands scattered far and wide, feeling the same warmth, this collective warmth. All this sweet love pouring and flowing your way.

Philip and I have lately been re-playing some of the times we've shared in the last twenty years. You really have been the vital spark behind what he and I have been able to do; without you being you, there could never have been an Island Institute. Thank you for understanding Philip and loving him the way you do. Thank you for so selflessly sharing him with me and with so many others. Thank you for your ability to recognize a dream and a vision when you see one. It takes one to know one.

I love your man, I love all your men…and I thought, again, as I sat there, of my promise to you. You know the one I mean. I'm good for this one, darling James.

Tomorrow is another day. Sweet dreams, sweet Jamien. God Bless, Tim and Sam and Jamie and Micah and Philip.

Love, Peter

Peter Ralston <ralston@midcoast.com>
Rockport, ME, USA - Monday, April 05, 1999 at 23:05:36 (EDT)

Networks of the Heart

. . . .

I do not know you.

You do not know me. I do, however,

know of you and these words

I must share. Your babies will grow

and carry on, and you will

live on in them. Be at peace,

for you've done your job well.

Anonymous, April 8, 1999

Wendy & Alex's Wedding Flag, 1978

Dear Jamie,

We were deeply saddened to learn from Geoff Getman that your illness had progressed. Years ago, when we learned about your illness, we knew it was a cosmic mistake.

You are a remarkable woman. While all of us possess spirit in greater or lesser degrees, you have developed your spirit into its fullness and, most importantly, you have shared your spirit with others. Jamie, we are all richer for your life. Carry your warrior spirit on your journey.

Peace, Virginia Wyly and Jack Allen

Virginia Wyly <Wylymv@BSCMAIL.Buffalostate.edu>
Buffalo, NY USA - Tuesday, April 06, 1999 at 08:28:55 (EDT)

Hi, Miss Morehouse!

I haven't seen you for awhile but you have never been very far from my thoughts. I just wanted to tell you that I was going through a box of school workbooks and papers that my mom has kept for me, and I came across a sandwich bag that had a piece of semi-recognizable honeycomb. It doesn't seem like long ago that, when as kindergarten kids, we went down to Vinalhaven to go bowling and visit the bee lady. I was so fascinated with those buzzing bees! I remember that it was a nice sunny day and that we had a great bag lunch at your parents' house.

Thank you for my first experiences. You made a BIG impression on my life. I told my husband about the greatest teacher I ever had and how lucky I was that our paths crossed. I hope that I can show my son things that he will remember when he is 28, just as you did me.

Love, Jessica
North Haven Community School, Kindergarten Class of 1977

Jessica MacDonald-Stearns <jstearns@sad7.k12.me.us>
North Haven, ME USA - Tuesday, April 06, 1999 at 09:16:36 (EDT)

Dearest Jamie,

   You remain in my thoughts constantly. I am filled with thoughts of love and radiance. Your image fills my heart and in this moment reminds me to dance, to sing, and to embrace each moment as a very precious gift.

   At the very same time I am filled with sadness that brings a heaviness to my heart and tears into my eyes. I feel a great love for you. I pray that you are comfortable and at peace and that your family is continually wrapped in love from the community that has loved you so dearly.

   Lucy Flight and I had tea yesterday. She brought the quilt that you had made for Nina. What beauty you have created. We celebrated you and sent our love.

Nancy M. Cray <nmcjps@seis.com>
Falmouth, ME USA - Tuesday, April 06, 1999 at 10:30:46 (EDT)

Sweet Jamien,

   I just learned of this "place" for you, and have been basking in it all morning. Then, thinking of you, I walked down to the boat house and found a wishing rock. It was warmed from the sun, with a perfect white ring linking stone, which reminded me of your strong spirit. I walked out on the dock and held the rock over water for a while, thinking that the water looks like green tea…should be green tea…an ocean of it…for Jamien, so that the gulls and loons could share in your tea ceremony as well. Your rock made a most wonderful "puh-luuunk" when tossed into the sea of green tea.

   I am glad for the visit we had a couple weekends ago. Even in physical weakness you are vibrant: a most beautiful, inspiring woman who grows moss table gardens and lives with a grateful heart. You--Jamien, Philip, Tim, Sam, Jamie, and Micah--are all in my thoughts.

   Much love, Amy

Amy Rawe <amy@hopemag.com>
Brooklin, ME USA - Tuesday, April 06, 1999 at 11:08:05 (EDT)

My Dearest Jamie,

   Remember this? You and Kelly and Janice and I were driving to some little-bitty town south of Warsaw, to celebrate St. Michael's Mass. It was a glorious day, and about a mile from the town we passed some farmers walking along the road, also going to the Mass? And we picked up all of them that could be crammed inside the van? And during the service, walking all the way around the outside of the church in the procession? And the colors of the women's (and the men's) Sunday best?

   And do you remember how wonderful it was to sit in the sidewalk restaurants along Nowy Swiat or Marszalkowska when spring finally exploded out of never-ending winter, and people were just mad to be outside? And the wonderful tulip beds in the parks--thousands of red tulips. And riding the tram out to Lazienki Park? What a time!

   My very dear friend, for me, you are one of my life's special people. Like minutes in a day, some few people you meet in life are the ones that give definition to all the rest. You have been one of those key people for me, and I am grateful for our time together. I cannot imagine what you have been through now and in these last many months, but I hope it is some consolation to you to know the impact you have had on so many others. You are regularly in our thoughts. We send you every bit of love one of these computers can hold.

   David, Beth, Erin, and Jamien

David Leckey <leckeyd@ibm.net>
Portland, OR USA - Tuesday, April 06, 1999 at 14:38:52 (EDT)

Dear Jamie,

   Although I don't know you, and was directed to your site by a friend, I wanted to say how moved I have been to read how profoundly and joyously you touched people's lives. It is an inspiration to me, and makes me want to

Jamien in Poland, 1974

live my own life with such generosity of spirit.

I was particularly touched by the note from the woman you gave your hat to--the intimacy and particularity of your gesture, and her humor. My thanks to you for your light.

Jackie Brookner

Jackie Brookner <JBrookn@aol.com>
NY, NY USA - Tuesday, April 06, 1999 at 15:18:50 (EDT)

I have a wonderful memory of Jamie from a Vinalhaven visit years ago. One of her boys, about age four or five, had his shoes on backwards. I learned that he liked them that way and was permitted to wear them that way. A rare mom. Lucky boys. Thinking of you, Jamie.

Lisa

lisa getman ellis
USA - Tuesday, April 06, 1999 at 17:37:19 (EDT)

DEAREST JAMIE,

   I have had wonderful visions of your sparkling eyes and beautiful smile since I received the invitation for tea. We go back to Adams School on the first day of kindergarten. Best little friends for so many years. You were so special and such a wonderful inspiration for me. I had so much fun playing at your house. Your adorable mother always had fun activities to do, baking or sewing or little nature adventures. Your school projects were always the best! Do you remember the Colonial doll? You designed an authentic soldier costume to fit on your doll. It had the boots and hat and everything.

   I pulled out the class of '69 yearbook in which you wrote to me, "Genuine friends never disappear--they only part for a while." I hope this message brings a little smile and warm thoughts. A gentle hug to you, Jamie.

   Love , Joyce Sullivan

Joyce Sullivan Murphy <jsmmurphy@aol.com>
Lexington, MA USA - Tuesday, April 06, 1999 at 17:42:34 (EDT)

DEAREST JAMIEN,

   I have been reading through your guestbook and am in awe at the content. It allows me to cry and feel my grief; for this I am grateful.

   I have a very clear memory of some time spent with you at Lawsonís quarry one hot summer day. You spoke to me with incredible honesty and clarity about your process with your illness. I thanked you then for sharing with me and reminding me of the preciousness of life every day! I am ever grateful to have known you and to have had the opportunity to be in your presence, however brief.

   Thank-you, and rest quietly soft, sweet Jamien.

   Love to you and your family, Martha

Martha Clayter <resonating@earthlink.net>
Camden, Me USA - Tuesday, April 06, 1999 at 18:49:50 (EDT)

Dear Jamie,

I'm thinking of what a force you are and have been and still will be. I got used to your being in the yoga room and then you couldn't be any longer. There was a big piece missing. I felt the same when you were not down in that front pew at church. You have carried a very palpable spiritual essence with you through this cancer journey. It gives us strength. My trying to adjust to your being removed from us presents itself in many forms, depending on the hour of the day, the time of year, the weather, what words I remember your having spoken to me. You are about to enter that higher realm, but I always felt that you were really on a higher plane than most of us on this earthly journey. I hope your leaving is as peaceful as your countenance. I will see you live on in Tim, Sam, James, and Micah, and I will remember that you were more excited for my becoming the grandmother of twins than most of my own family was!

With great love and wishes for a peaceful, useful journey now, Sue Crane

Susan Crane <craneski@midcoast.com>
USA - Tuesday, April 06, 1999 at 22:19:26 (EDT)

Dear Jamien,

Matt's name means "Gift of God," and one of the divine treasures I've received, thanks to him, is our friendship… How lucky for me that Matt and Micah were together each year starting in kindergarten! That I could get to know you, a woman whose writing I'd admired from afar, and sip tea with you in your kitchen, eat picnics on the rocks of a sparkling quarry, drink cider in my van on the way to the Haunted Halloween walk…

I have learned so much from your creative, loving example. How to make the ordinary special. ("It's just a paper bag," you said to me in February. But you magically transformed it into a lovely Valentine.) How to

Jamie and Micah modeling their mother's hats, 1998

make the mundane mom stuff sacred--like piling the kids off to Miss Plum's to commemorate their last day of school. (Remember the excitement in their sticky, smiling faces?) Your practical tips for surviving the endless baseball games and practices, rainy April Saturdays, and so much more.

And, of course, the gift none of us can fathom--your transformation of the terrible and terrifying into a journey of love, hope, and gratitude.

I know that I am blessed to call you my friend. One day I'll join you "on the other side" and we'll laugh, listen to opera, and wear great hats together. In the meantime, I'll treasure your lessons, my memories, and Matt's twin buddies.

God's peace and love to you, Philip, Tim, Sam, Jamie, and Micah.

With love, Vicki

Vicki Doudera <doudera5@midcoast.com>
Camden, ME USA - Tuesday, April 06, 1999 at 23:13:23 (EDT)

Jamien and twins with Hurricane Island Outward Bound mothers, Rockport, 1989

DEAR JAMIEN MOREHOUSE AND PHILIP CONKLING,

You will think I am a nut, but, at the request of Elizabeth Martin, I have been offering prayers for your family and ancestors. My parents both passed away from cancer, and I am very happy for you that you have arranged this wonderful Web site for people to express their love and feelings to all of you. I was so moved by the letters that I just had to drop a note myself and say that I cannot imagine how much your friendships have enriched others.

   Death is always an unknown, and I wish you just the very best trip home. I don't wish to sound corny or insincere, and I apologize for any intrusion, for I just wanted to respond to the beautiful way in which people are being allowed to communicate and share their reflections, great stories, and most of the all, their love.

   With continued prayers for you, Jamien and Philip, most sincerely yours,
   Dale Richardson

Dale Richardson <dalerich@flash.net>
East Boston, MA USA - Tuesday, April 06, 1999 at 23:36:16 (EDT)

April 7

Today Jamien was asleep more than she was awake. Her energy is pulling in from her edges and moving toward her center. In the end, isn't it the way it should be--that what is left at the end of life is the energy of the heart.

DEAR JAMIEN,

   One day in Damariscotta, I ran into you at the Rising Tide. You looked wonderful and I asked what you were doing? You replied, "I don't eat anymore."

   That was quite some time ago. And since Saturday, I have been marveling at the mystery of your continued life. This morning I woke thinking of the French phrase for how lovers exist: *l'eau et l'air fraiche* (water and fresh air), and it explained it to me as well what I've learned from the privilege of visiting this site: your life has been about the overflowing merriment of love of life. May you and your generous family always be in that irrepressibly bubbly place, as you always will be in each of our hearts.

This site reflects how immensely it is returned. Thank you and bon voyage.

Aviva Rahmani <ghostnet@foxislands.net>
Vinalhaven, Me USA - Wednesday, April 07, 1999 at 10:05:43 (EDT)

Jamie and Micah's second birthday party, 1990

DEAR JAMIE,

My love and prayers are with you. Your courage and faith are a beautiful thing. What can there be to fear if you face the greatest fear of all with such grace? I wish I knew you better--but there will be "worlds enough and time" on the other side.

Sarah Morehouse <ssm2491@siena.edu>
Poughkeepsie, NY USA - Wednesday, April 07, 1999 at 11:43:56 (EDT)

DEAR JAMIEN,

You slip into my thoughts so often these days and even into my dreams. I wanted you to know that last week I watched the fifth graders performing their dances, the culmination of a week-long residency at Rockport Elementary School. I watched your Micah and my Ned and was so proud and honored to be there. I imagined being eyes for you, as so many of us will be as time goes by.

Jamien, I have had to reorganize some files at Peopleplace so the one you so aptly labeled "Credit Card Rinky-doo" can be in the front of the crummy file cabinet, just to make me laugh.

I love you. Lee

Lee Lingelbach <lwling@mint.net>
Hope, ME USA - Wednesday, April 07, 1999 at 14:08:43 (EDT)

Dearest Jamie,

The first time I remember meeting you was at Pat's house. A new little visitor, your Tim, greeted our little playgroup. Your and Tim's visits always brought new energy and joy to the toddling children and chatting moms. All of us rearing our first children and clinging to any and all profound tips to aid this "parenting thing."

We've added more children and more wisdom to our lives. Your strength and courage to raise your family of boys so unto themselves has influenced my resolve to embrace the diversity in my own children and those I touch on a daily basis.

I so enjoyed those first-grade plays in Miss Crawford's room, starring Hillory and Tim. Mostly for the chance that you'd have the twins with you and I could snag one to coddle and bounce. I'd pass my new baby off to his dad and eagerly reach for one of your babies as you made your entrance, all askew from those wriggling bundles. Joseph's new friends, yet their sideline positions certainly didn't last long, did they. Just look at these boys!

Both our Sams will carve their paths in life with an unusually large wake. It must be the name--Go for it, guys!! Little Sam thanks you for the book at Christmas. He refuses to let me pack it away with all the other holiday reads. When asked, he says it came from "The Conkling Mom."

Behind you, across vast distances of space and time, from the places you've left, we will sense your presence through our memories and in your family. They are but fragile perfections of this earthly world.

As I've said so often, I will be there for the boys, whether it be to return something Jamie has forgotten or to give a pep talk, they are part of us.

Love, Maureen

Jamie and Micah's third birthday party, 1991

Maureen <predham@midcoast.com>
Camden, ME USA - Wednesday, April 07, 1999 at 14:43:47 (EDT)

Jamien at Hat Show to benefit New Hope for Women, 1998

Dear Jamie,

I am remembering some of the times we've shared and realizing that every time I ever spent with you was so special to me. I'm remembering a balmy June day and our long talk on our drive to and from Portland, where we heard Deepak Chopra speak at USM [University of Southern Maine] years ago. I remember the wonderful picnic that you had thought to pack for us. You always create beauty in the simplest of moments! I remember singing with you and other women, swapping songs, and laughing.

I'm thinking of the times I've felt your passion through reading your work in the paper and all of the special projects you have been involved with for our community and especially our children. I love seeing your beautiful family at church, or marching with the scouts, or juggling, and you always there loving them. I remember the Friendship Feast and you washing dishes in the church kitchen, working at your own special party. You've given me encouragement as you have given so much to countless others. I'll always remember you and your tremendous loving heart. I have one last song to sing to you.

> Be like a bird who, pausing in her flight
> On a limb too slight, feels it give way beneath her,
> But sings, sings, knowing she has wings...
> Sings, sings, knowing she has wings!

Safe journey my sister. Love, Linda Z

Linda Zeigler <rounder@midcoast.com>
Camden, Me USA - Wednesday, April 07, 1999 at 14:59:16 (EDT)

Dear Aunt Jamie,

I remember going to your hat show. That's where we made the hats and I bought that hat, I mean the crown. I liked the crown that I made. Remember when we went there with Carrick and Skyler. That's all I want to say right now.

    love, Tucker

    [Bruce Morehouse's son, age five]

TUCKER <baggedmail@acadia.net>
Belfast, ME USA - Wednesday, April 07, 1999 at 16:55:48 (EDT)

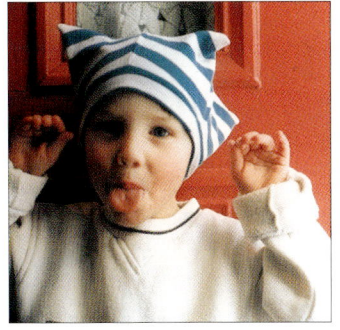

Tucker Morehouse modeling his aunt's hat, 1998

    Hi, my name is Skylar, and I am Michael Kelly's son. He sent me an e-mail about this Web page telling me that you are a friend of his. I wanted to say that I am really sorry about the fact that you have cancer and I hope that you can fight it off. I also think that the tea thing is really neat!

    With best wishes, Skylar T. Kelly

Skylar Kelly <pauleigh@javanet.com>
Brunswick, ME USA - Wednesday, April 07, 1999 at 17:26:21 (EDT)

DEAR JAMIEN,

    I don't know you, but I want to thank you for using the Web for a truly meaningful purpose.

    Dying with dignity is no mean trick, and I have the deepest respect for those who can bring it off (my mother set an example that I hope to live up to). The fact that you can open up the process on a public medium like this and share it with others is, I think, an act of personal courage and a gift to all who discover you. Thank you. I'm only sorry I won't get a chance to meet you in person.

David Taylor <dtaylor@engines.com>
San Mateo, CA USA - Wednesday, April 07, 1999 at 18:10:28 (EDT)

DEAR JAMIEN,

Friends seem to orbit in circles, with those circles growing, fusing, changing, overlapping...I feel privileged to have had the opportunity to pass occasionally into your amazing circle and can't but wish it had happened more often.

This Web site is a beautiful confirmation of all that I sensed in you and more--an amazing woman who is inspirational, creative, committed, caring, loving, strong, passionate, intelligent. You have touched so many people and places with your spirit. At Peopleplace there are gentle reminders of your presence everywhere. Your dedication to children and your wonderful way with them is something I will always treasure, as a mother and as a friend.

Thank you for your light. It will always shine brightly in my heart.

With love, Karyn

Karyn Bresnahan <karynb@tidewater.net>
Hope, ME USA - Wednesday, April 07, 1999 at 21:19:42 (EDT)

Jamien, ca. 1980

JAMIEN,

    Though I am speaking from my own heart,
    I know I express the sentiments of many...
    Your creative and energetic spirit
    has infused so many of us!
    You have inspired us with your delightful way of
    looking at the world
    ...always with fresh and perceptive eyes
    those beautiful light brown eyes!
    Applying your endlessly creative hand and mind
    to a myriad of forms and materials
    transforming a joyous heart

to Joyous Art;
Appreciating the beauty in everyday things,
and finding remarkable ways to breathe
a vibrant new life
full of promise, color, and fun
into the old or cast-off;
Caring deeply for our Environment,
our community
and the individuals in it,
and especially the children;
Caring enough to teach us all
how better to appreciate and nurture
everything and everyone that makes up our world;
Seeking out and sharing the humor and delight
in the odd corners of life,
and finding it where others might least expect it
(take head lice, for example!);
Rarely satisfied with the status quo,
you wring the most out of Life's experiences,
especially for your family
and your boys.
You understand, as few do, what really matters in Life
(--Hand and Heart--)
then, with resolve,
you buck the media countercurrent
to bring home, with fun and humor, lessons on
Life's true riches!
Jamien,
You bring to the lives of all you touch

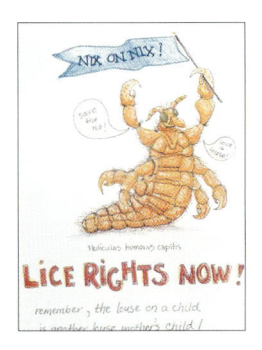

more color, depth, and humor
than we ourselves can find
…and so, you inspire us to look harder
to discover those qualities
within ourselves.
YOU are a Nurturer, a Generator!

"That which came to you as seed
goes to the next as blossom
and that which came to you as blossom
goes on as fruit." (adapted from Dawna Markova)

Thank you for enriching our lives,
forever,
in uncountable ways.
With a great deal of love, respect, and gratitude
and the deepest desire for your comfort
and wish for your healing,

Anita…and the Uncountable Many.

Anita Brosius-Scott <scotts@mint.net>
Camden, ME USA - Wednesday, April 07, 1999 at 21:32:34 (EDT)

DEAR JAMIE,

Your courage and humor about your cancer have been such an inspiration to me. More than that, however, I have been inspired by your unique approach to your art. You have been whimsical, spontaneous, and thoughtful all at once. Your story about the Yellow Woman paintings was a great one. It simmered in my subconscious for several months and suddenly popped out in a series of monotypes I was working on about a year ago. I was quite surprised to see it. It was like having you drop by. I know you'll show up again in my work.

   Till then, much love, Kate Mahoney

Kate Mahoney <bcphoto@maine.rr.com>
Yarmouth, ME USA - Wednesday, April 07, 1999 at 22:31:19 (EDT)

DEAR JAMIEN,
   We think of you as we watch your mackerel turn slowly, hanging over our kitchen table. The first time we met you and the twins, on one of our first trips to Vinalhaven, catching a ride on the Island Institute boat from Vinalhaven to North Haven for the lobster boat races, we thought you were pretty cool.
   Then swimming lessons, circuses, night soccer games, moonlight chi qong and--the story I will one day write--qi gong at the quarry, led by Jamien, with a half dozen or so of her sisters in spirit, while their children froze their @!!*&% off. What a spirit. You are always an integral part of Vinalhaven for us. Much love and wishes for a peaceful journey,
   Munch, George, Max, and Joanna

Munch Grogan and family <jomax@mediaone.net>
Watertown, MA USA - Wednesday, April 07, 1999 at 22:31:27 (EDT)

DEAR JAMIE,
   How well I remember the day...You were in Boston for extended cancer treatment and you came all the way over to the Museum of Fine Arts just to meet me and tell me how much my son, John, meant to your family. How

47

incredibly thoughtful of you at a time when so much was going on in your life! So many people would not have spared the time or the energy to make such an effort. *[John "Woody" Woodward was the boys' "house-sitter" after school for a month in 1995. Woody taught Sam Conkling how to juggle.]*

    I remember that there was a wonderful air of serenity about you. It was immediately clear that your unbeatable spirit, courage, and positive energy provided a powerful gift for all those whose lives you touched. I am grateful to you for reaching out to John and drawing him close. Sharing your love, your wisdom, and your family with him is a gift he will always treasure. We will be forever grateful for your generosity. Ron and I hold you and your family in our hearts and send all of you our love.

Jean Woodward <jeanandron@AOL.com>
Marblehead, MA USA - Wednesday, April 07, 1999 at 23:59:31 (EDT)

April 8
• • • •

If it is more blessed to give than to receive, then receiving so much blessedness may someday teach us graceful gratefulness. May it be so. In the early morning light of this graying day, Jamien opened a gift from a group of friends to find her own namesake has now been etched onto a star in the heavens. To find her star, you must first look for Polaris, where Jamien's compass has always pointed, and then drop your sights towards Cassiopeia's sharp angles in the dark sky to find the constellation called Camelopardalis. And shimmering a million light years out there is a star named Jamien, faint but radiant, forever fixed when the moon does not eclipse her light.

48

Dear Jamie,

your nun picture hangs over my bed. it will keep us both safe.

love, sara

sara gilfenbaum <sarag@sad50.k12.me.us>
thomaston, me USA - Thursday, April 08, 1999 at 07:25:10 (EDT)

Dearest Jamien,

Your boys are doing such a wonderful job on this Web site. Once again, you must be very proud of them!

The lovely photos of you are a treasure to see and I find so many other snapshots coming to mind. Sitting around the fire on the Close Enough hillside on one of those glorious Vermont summer evenings. A photo of a jubilant you and your friend in Poland riding across a country paddock on a motorcycle (or was that a giant pig?).

Miranda and I went up to the Cathedral of St. John the Divine for the Easter Sunday service. We arrived just as the Bishop, all mitered and robed, was knocking on the outside of the big doors with his crook. Slowly and creakily the doors opened, the State Bombard Trumpets blasted everyone out of their seats, and we followed him for miles down the aisle. The altar was a glorious vision of Easter lilies, shimmering gold and silver, and billowing incense. Magical sounds from Judy Collins, Paul Winter, and the choir echoed across the stones. We said lots of prayers for you and felt you there with us throughout.

A cup of hot green tea was sipped on Monday at 4:00, sitting in the garden at the Museum. The trees are just beginning to glow with that early spring chartreuse, so it was a great pleasure to be there and enjoy. It was also a special joy to think of sharing the tea with you this year (because I really did imagine you sitting there on the Mexican star-burst garden seat next to me), and to think of all the teas in past years and even in the ones to come. It will always be an honored tradition.

In the meantime, Jamien, I embrace you with a warm hug and send you my love. Deborah

Deborah Shinn <shinnde@ch.si.edu>
New York, NY USA - Thursday, April 08, 1999 at 10:39:03 (EDT)

Dear Jamie,

Our paths have crossed several times, on Hurricane Island, at the old IGA, Market Basket, and generally about town. This life in the midcoast seems like a wonderful web, overlaying meetings and glimpses of another's life. And like any web, the movements and tugs of one part pull the other parts.

While walking with some Easter fairies on the wooded path to Mount Battie, I came to understand that you were "sailing on." I was saddened and thought of the places our lives have touched. Another friend shared this Web and I was honored to read so much beauty.

I also want to tell you and your family of a true sense of Grace that radiates around you and I feel blessed to have seen this Web used in such a holy way. Many times in my life I have sat with family and friends as they die, and I can feel the soul of the person making the room a sacred place. Using the Web for you has extended this--I feel the sacred and the holy as I read the words here. I feel the sacred and the holy as I write my own words here, and my life is better because of this gift of your family and you. Bless you.

Love, Jeff

jeff powell <jeffpowell@altavista.net>
Camden, me USA - Thursday, April 08, 1999 at 11:16:02 (EDT)

Spring greetings! The global community is small and the challenges we face often universal. I just had a note from a classmate from Harvard
informing me about this page to share hopes and challenges. Jay, I know, has been in closer touch than I have. I am, of course, younger (my birth was an afterthought on Moon Hill) and thus never really knew the older gang. Yet, my thoughts are with you all--Dick, Lee, Jamie, Bruce, and company. I was married this past fall, and through my wife I also have been part of a tough family battle with cancer as her mother fights to stay alive. So as new flowers emerge each day, I hope the spring brings some light to the beauty and not just the pain of life.

All the best, Minky

Charlie Abelmann <CAbelmann@WorldBank.org>
Washington, DC USA - Thursday, April 08, 1999 at 10:32:18 (EDT)

Bruce, Dick, Lee, and Jamien Morehouse, New Hampshire, ca. 1979

JAMIE,

Last night the girls and I went to a fundraising community event and concert to raise money for Kosovo aid. I sat next to a woman in a huge pink flowerpot of a hat with a lone and equally huge sunflower bursting from it. And it was you, with all the hats and hearts you have made and inspired.

One strong and beautiful older woman read from an ancient story of the Sabine women, who, in despair over a senseless war killing their fathers and husbands and children, took their children out onto the fields of war between the fighters and caused their eyes and hearts to open and the fighting to cease--and you were there in your boldness and vision.

This same woman then read from her own poetry, including an ode to her

51

Poker night, New Year's Eve, 1998

son, a portrait from his cradle days when she sat before dawn, nursing him and watching shadows give way to shapes…and years later opening a letter from him thanking her for being the fountain of life that she was, even forgiving her the time she spent in jail for protesting the Vietnam war. And there you were again! A strong and loving mother: vibrant and crazy and full of the unexpected, such a magnet for that part in each of us that responds to vitality as flowers to the sun. You're moving on now, as you must. You're not leaving us, you're changing. Thank you for your work and your play. We are richer and our hearts more full of love for you, and, we pray, each other. Though I write through tears, I feel blessed again.

Bodies, who needs 'em…! Tino

tino obrien <Ddude22@aol.com>
montpelier, Vt USA - Thursday, April 08, 1999 at 11:55:01 (EDT)

Thank you for sharing this time with those of us who think of you often and send you our love and energy. I have wanted to somehow connect with you without pulling your energy away from where you need it. This is perfect. I also want to pass on news about the the Wednesday morning qi gong practice. As was your vision, we will begin dancing at the Camden Library Ampitheater next week, weather permitting. I know your spirit will always be with us as we do the twelve movements of Yuan Ji Dance.

Sheila Tasker <tasker@midcoast.com>
Tenants Harbor, ME USA - Thursday, April 08, 1999 at 11:53:39 (EDT)

Dear Jamien,

I was so happy to join in the great tradition of Jamien's tea this past Monday. Everyone raised a cup to you. In fact your spirit has infused every local moment. Whether it be a walk, a cup of tea, a meeting, or a phone call, it is a community vigil in this chapter of your beautiful journey. You are dearly loved! I think of you in yoga and how you and your life have stretched and inspired and strengthened our sense of fun, of play, of courage, and have energized us all. I am grateful to be a part of what you've given us. My thoughts are with you and your family.

   With love, Hilary

Hilary Carr <crabbit@midcoast.com>
Camden, Me USA - Thursday, April 08, 1999 at 11:49:14 (EDT)

DEAR JAMIE,

   You are in my thoughts constantly, hoping you are comfortable and peaceful. I am missing being able to talk with you, but I am thankful for years full of laughter, chocolate bake-offs, the Florida drive and pulling boat time, b-day parties, poker, christenings, your inspiration as a mother and creator of family friendships, art of all kinds, dump lady, and so much more. A great friend, teacher to me, and a grand lover and liver of life in entirety. Thank you, Jamien, for being such an important part of my life. Thank you, Philip, Tim, Sam, Jamie, and Micah for sharing your wonderful wife and mom. Fair winds, fair tides on your journey.

   Love to you all, Wendy

wendy weiler
USA - Thursday, April 08, 1999 at 16:48:58 (EDT)

   I do not know you. You do not know me. I do, however, know of you and these words I must share…From what I know, you have left this place better than you found it. Your babies will grow and carry on, and you will live on in them. Be at peace, be at peace, be at peace, for you've done your job well, very well indeed. Even people who don't know you know this much for sure.

   God Bless. Anonymous

Anonymous
USA - Thursday, April 08, 1999 at 14:04:36 (EDT)

April 9
• • • •

The nights are long and sometimes hard for Jamien, although sleep comes and carries away her cares. Today Jamien had a great day starting with a visit from Carol Rohl. Carol is an exquisite harpist and asked Jamien if she could leave her harp in the corner of her room and that she would arrive unpredictably for what Jamien calls "drive-by harping." Carol stayed throughout the morning, which also included acupuncture and Reiki sessions. Jamien got such a lift from the morning's angels that she was able to get out onto the porch where she said she felt like she was on an ocean liner in a deck chair. A little like heaven on earth. So for today, all is well.

DEAR JAMIE,

   I joined you for Tea Monday at 4:00 p.m. I took the dog and my travel mug and started out at about 3:45. I wanted to be as deep into Drummer Hill woods as possible before the appointed time. The trails through Drummer Hill are all on Keene Public Land just minutes from busy Court Street. I carried you with me up the steep grade on the woods road, which turns rocky now and then where spring rains have hollowed gullies.

   I sipped my tea sitting there and thought of the dozens of people all quietly doing the same, all gathered around your bed. Your dining-turned-bedroom magically expanded to make room for all of us. Let me tell you what I saw. From my log I saw a blur of blue-gray beech wood saplings. The afternoon sun glinted off the parched teardrops of dried beech leaves as they clung here and there to their trees. Straight up the hill, though no path points it out, sits a cellar hole lined with stone. It's barely bigger than your hospital bed and there is an outline of what was once a chimney. Maybe a sugar house, though there are hardly enough maples nearby to warrant it. Maybe a solitary cabin like the tea house Philip built for you. It's pleasant to go there and look out toward the west.

   The dog whined "Why?" when I stayed overlong on the log so I continued on, tea mug in hand. The path crosses the power line and the hilly view opened out to the hills west of Keene--the opposite bank of the lake that sparkled here in ancient times. Spruce and pine thrust up here and there on either side and I could just see the white trails of Mt. Ascutney Ski Area on the rounded blue knob in the distance. I carried you with me all the way to Goose Pond. We saw a tangle of birches, their red buds making a purple filigree against the blue sky. A pine tree still waved its branches, head thrown back to the sky, never looking down at the mighty gashes in its trunk drilled by the pileated woodpecker. I drank the last of my tea at the shore of the lovely watering place that is Goose Pond. No geese visited there on Monday, but I watched the white-water skid of several landing ducks, glad to be back at last in their favorite place. The sun was lowering and we turned back for home. On the way I found the most exquisite piece of birch bark, thin and delicate yet strong and resilient. On it I wrote, "Jamien was here."

   Much love to you on your journey. Love, Susan

Susan Murata <toby@cheshire.net>
Keene, NH USA - Friday, April 09, 1999

Dear Jamie and Company,

I do not know if you will remember me but I visited you on the Island of Vinalhaven. I am the fourteen-year-old son of Joel Magnuson and Kim Morehouse/Magnuson. I thank you for giving me a tour of the island and house. It was the neatest part of my '98 summer vacation. After we all settled in to a couple of sandwiches, we all piled into Uncle Dick's station wagon and went to the quarry. That was a great place, with its crystal clear water, rock sides, and zip-line. When we went back to the house we all dried off and than you gave me a tour of the attic. That was cool! There were boxes of old artifacts that the people who had dug around the house left, and the table with the art supplies all over it. We then went downstairs and looked at all of Dick's "stick snakes."

Then we went to the buoy tree. (This, of course, was after we had gone down to the shore to see what treasures were in store for us.) Not long afterwards we had to go back to the mainland on the ferry we had come over on. I thank you again for making that trip about as memorable a trip as I could experience.

My wishes go out to you in your time of strife and battle. Thank you ever so much for the memories.

Love you, Kyle Magnuson and the Magnuson Family

Kyle Magnuson <Jmagnu@together.net>
Fairfax, Vt USA - Friday, April 09, 1999

Dear Jamien,

I woke up very early yesterday morning, something like 3:30 a.m., thinking of you and your family. I prayed for you: for peace, for rest, for a full knowing of the love of so many, but especially of God's love for you. Thinking about you then lead me to pray for almost everyone I love in my life…that kept me busy till it was time to get up!

I've written you three letters so far, but haven't sent a one. Seems like each time the words hold less oomph for what I would like to say. Knowing you as a Peopleplace mom and mover & shaker was a blessing for me. What a superb example for all of us moms and dads out here. Watching you parent so attentively, so intentively (probably not a real word) was a great gift. The Peopleplace community and this community at large have been so touched, so changed, so encouraged, and so inspired by your loving kindnesses.

I join the many out here praying for you, God's speed.

Love, Kathleen

Kathleen VandenBrink <bvanden@mint.net>   Friday, April 09, 1999

Jamie and Micah, mackerel fishing, Vinalhaven, 1993

DEAR JAMIEN,

Oh, such love in these messages! I hope you let them wrap around you like a Navajo blanket whose beauty is an honest reflection of the symbols of life.

We have shared tea for so many years. I feel so honored to be your friend. Our children have donned seaweed loin cloths and run hand and hand to lighthouses. We have laughed and explored and embraced beauty and love.

I want you to know that the pennants with your hand design that you gave to my children so many years ago have always traveled with us on sailing trips. They have been flown over Guadeloupe, Dominica, New Zealand, and the Islands of Tonga, as well as Penobscot Bay.

Your hand, Jamien, your heart, have touched more people than you will ever know.

With love, June

June LaCombe <jlacombe@maine.rr.com>
Pownal, Me USA - Friday, April 09, 1999

Dear Jamie,

   Only someone like you could figure out a way to use technology to advance matters of the heart and spirit! It has been a rare and intimate privilege to read the amazing letters to you from all the corners of your life. Thank you for welcoming all of us, even many who have yet to know you, into this darkest and brightest of times for you and your family.

   At tea time on Monday, I went down by the shore of Damariscotta Lake at Camp Kieve, where I was working. There was a blown-down pine which made a perfect perch from which to celebrate your magnificent life and light and spirit. I was filled with great joy and deep sadness and ultimately a sense of calm. That only came when you swooped by, in the form of a striking adult bald eagle, just returned to the open waters of the lake now that the ice is out. That eagle was you…I caught you winking at me!

   All love to you and your family, Kit Pfeiffer

Kit Pfeiffer <maae@acadia.net>
cushing, me USA - Friday, April 09, 1999

Jamien…

   Your triumph of love is that you have become this love. And this gives you a freedom even vaster than the mystics dare hope. Most spiritual paths say that when you leave the body, you also leave all attachment. It is not so.

   When love is perfected in a wise soul, such attachments can become channels of creativity, in which you can always reach out to give and receive love. This is not clinging; it is grace. It is rarely spoken about, rarely attained. But it happens. You are not leaving those you love, but bringing them along in your illumined heart.

   Guys, please trust this. Many people will tell you that your Mom is a saint. It is true, and you must trust what this means for you. She became a saint out of love for you. It means she carved a spiritual channel between herself and each one of you in which you can always reach her, receive her love, and help her to grow by giving her your love and your best courage. Please trust this. It is rare, but it is real. If you don't give in to cynicism, but dare to trust in the power behind her love, you will find that that power is real. This comes with my love and prayers. And to you, Jamien, total awe and love!

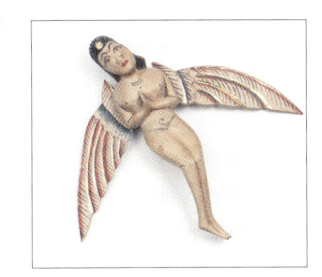

Cynthia Bourgeault <treaven@saltspring.com>
Salt Spring Island , BC Canada - Friday, April 09, 1999

Dear Jamie,

   I have a memory I want to share with you, Philip, and your beloved boys. Two summers ago, you and I were sitting on the ferry en route to Vinalhaven. Richard and Philip were elsewhere on the boat with our respective sons, and we had some quiet time together. You were working on a beautiful peach and green quilt, which you had designed as a baby gift for a teacher. It bore the handprint of each child in her class. You were not well and I thought of the effort that you must have expended in secretly gathering the children and steadying all of their eager, sticky hands. I wanted to ask you about your health but I was shy and afraid for you. I was also afraid to confront my own greatest fear that I would lose one of my children or they would lose me. Finally, I simply asked you how you were feeling. You paused for a moment, needle in hand. You looked out over the bay and mentioned something about your alternative healing regimen. You were silent for a moment and pensive. Then you turned to me and fixed me with your beautiful eyes and said, "I feel lucky." I will never forget that.

   With all our love, Clare, Richard, Harry, Jacob, & Alice

Clare Tully <claretully@hotmail.com>
Tenafly, NJ - Friday, April 09, 1999

[Clare Tully is the wife of Richard Podolsky, one of the original staff members of the Island Institute.]

Dear Jamie,

A picture of you has been in my mind often over the years, especially since that day last summer when Alex and I ran into you at the Country Inn and you told me how challenging life had become. It was one of our earlier visits to the Rockaway. We were gathered together in that wonderful, sunny kitchen, your family all around. You were in the rocking chair, Micah to one breast, Jamie to the other. Tim and Sam were playing a game nearby on the floor. You were so at ease in your roles: nurturer, comforter, knowledgeable teacher knowing when to guide or umpire and when lessons were better learned on one's own. You never missed a beat and were so sensitive to all around you. I was in awe; still am; always will be.

I know, quite well in fact, a man who proudly proclaims you as his first love, when he was not much older than Tim on that day so long ago. Not surprising; with such kindness and sincere attention, what little boy could help himself.

Peace and love to you and your family, Sheri, Jason, and Alex

Sheri <slrd@foxislands.net>
Vinalhaven, ME USA - Friday, April 09, 1999

I just learned of this special Web site. I am a two-year breast cancer survivor, age 40, with two sons, ages four and two and a half. Reading about Jamien has given me such inspiration. I only wish I could of been touched by this special angel and her friendship before she was called to the heavenly light. God bless her family; my thoughts and prayers are with them. I only hope in my fight with this disease that I find her courage and strength and beautiful grace.

Robin Graham <Robinted@aol.com>
Terryville, CT USA - Friday, April 09, 1999

Dear Jamien,

Each morning I make myself a cup of tea and sit before the warmth of our woodstove. It's a time of prayer, reflection, and reading. You and your family have been much in my thoughts and prayers.

The letter I got from you three weeks ago is something I will save forever for its courage and the beauty of its honesty. Yours is a voice my children need to hear. At the dead center of darkness, your loving acceptance of the cards of life is something I'll never forget.

I've been thinking of those words, and your life, and the gift of this Web site. At night we sit quietly and read the beauty and the depth of all that is coming your way. It is so clear that your fearless life has caught so many people. And now, at this most difficult of times, all whom you caught, all the love you have given, is coming back to you.

You are in our thoughts and prayers. May God give you and your family comfort and peace.

Love, Chris and Kate Burr

Chris Burr <cburr@burr-assoc.com>
Dedham, MA USA - Friday, April 09, 1999

I first saw your Web site three days ago, when a friend drew my attention to it. I had trouble with such a personal situation on such a public medium. The intervening three days have been such a process: driving the turnpike in tears; stages of anger, denial, looking at dealing with death; recalling times with you. My fairly brief experience with the Internet has been mainly for business, mostly messages with attorneys or looking up facts. Very grounded. And here are these AMAZING, POWERFUL messages, many from familiar writers. I always think of you as so creative and such a teacher. And here you are, creating and teaching with your last breaths! All so overwhelming, in the full sense of the word. Thank you.

The black and white print of sheep-shearing you made when you first returned from Poland is next to my loom. So now must be the time to get the loom going again.

Thank you for so much, and thank you for the opportunity to say goodbye, queen with red shoes.

Love, Liz

Liz Hunter <titles@maine.rr.com>
Portland, Me. USA - Friday, April 09, 1999 at 20:45:18 (EDT)

Dear Family all,

I have to thank you for this site. I have signed on every night--I think, to feel a part of this incredible circle of friends, to share in the outpouring of love for a most remarkable person. Summer time spent at Rockaway has been such a memorable part of my life. It is life at its best, removed from the distractions of the modern world, a place to rejoice in the simple pleasures of life, and to enjoy the closeness of family. Best of all has been gathering around the dinner table at the end of a busy day, starting off with grace, holding hands and singing the grace:

   Tireless Guardian of our way,
   Thou has kept us well this day,
   While we thank thee we request
   Care continued, pardon, rest.
   (Squeeze!!)

Then the stories and laughter would begin, and how often the stories were yours, Jamie. How wonderful it is to laugh. And the singing! You know so many songs. Special times and special memories.

Thanks. Barb

P.S. Even though I'm so far away, I feel close by being able to see your wonderful face on this site. Thinking of you ALL, every day.

Barbara Harris <BarbHarr@aol.com>
Basking Ridge, NJ USA - Friday, April 09, 1999 at 22:21:28 (EDT)

Sam, Jamien, Micah, Philip, Jamie, and Tim, Rockaway, Lane's Island, 1988

DEAR JAMIE,

One of your hats, the Jester one, hangs among a collection I have from foreign countries. I treasure it because I think of you when I concentrate on it. You were in a writing class, led by Ruth, with me. Your presentations were profound. I particularly remember the one about your grandmother as a collector, and loved it. I'm in this age bracket and was delighted with your description of her talent. She gives me courage.

Eight years ago I had breast cancer. I'm so sad to be losing a sister, but grateful for the way you have lived with your illness.

I will miss your smile and your positive attitude in the face of your disease.

I think of you as I invite other women into my home to share tea and share your story. You, your family, mom, and dad are in my prayers.

    Love, Elva Hunt, summer resident

Elva Hunt <lillitan@ibm.net>
Asheville, NC USA - Friday, April 09, 1999 at 23:18:40 (EDT)

April 10 *It was a blustery, blowy day here as a strong northerly wind contested for the day's airs. But still we set up a deck chair on the porch and Jamien came out and watched the rolling main for over an hour. The light was alternately brilliantly shimmering and darkly shadowed. We lined her chair up with the bird feeder, and listened to a pair of mourning doves who sounded like the dispossessed souls of lovers lost at sea. Maybe it wasn't the* **Queen Mary,** *nor was it the* **Titanic;** *still, it was a bracing time on deck until pellets of hail drove her back inside. The rest of the day was quieter and ended with Garrison Keillor's annual joke show on "***The Prairie Home Companion.**"

GOOD MORNING JAMIEN,

    The sun is baking the island today, deep blue sky as far as the eye can see. I was thrilled to hear you had a chance to "lounge" on the porch yesterday. Soaking up the sun's rays and letting it fill your body with warmth and peace. I have never sat on an ocean liner deck chair, but taken in small doses, I think I could get used to it.

    I love the idea of the drive-by harping; I'm sure it fills your room with a wonderful sound. You have pampered us with your love and spirit; there is no reason not to have a drive-by harpist or take a spin on an ocean liner deck chair.

    I called the house yesterday and was pleasantly surprised to hear Micah's voice on the other end. Even though our talk was short, he seemed to be in good spirits. I miss the boys very much. They are etched in my heart and the times we spent juggling, playing, laughing, cavorting, etc. live on in me.

I hope you are enjoying some of the sunshine and warmth we have here on the island. Your deck chair awaits! Today is another day. My peaceful thoughts and prayers for you, Jamien and Philip, and the boys.

All my love, Woody

John H. "Woody" Woodward <woodward@ecology.coa.edu>
Bar Harbor, ME USA - Saturday, April 10, 1999 at 09:52:37 (EDT)

DEAR JAMIE,

My thoughts and prayers are with you and your family. Hey friend, we go back a long way, almost twenty-five years. Dayle, you, and I were quite the threesome. I remember all the get-togethers, picnics, long walks, and long talks.

I always knew you would be a wonderful mother. You were always so great with my kids, before you even had any of your own. The birthday party you had for Jason out to Rockaway, the apron you made for Jada on her fourth birthday, which her daughter now proudly wears.

Whatever you did, you gave it your best shot. Remember the time we went to the turkey shoot up in "Geeze" field and you beat out all those guys and won first prize? Then a few days later you had about a dozen of us out to Rockaway for dinner--the first-prize turkey!

I know that sometime we will see each other again, sit down to a cup of tea, and talk over old times.

Your Friend Forever, Cynthia

Cynthia Young <rambo@foxislands,net>
Vinalhaven, Me. USA - Saturday, April 10, 1999 at 09:53:03 (EDT)

Sam, the juggler man, 1998

DEAR JAMIEN,

Just checking in again! This page has grown so much since I first saw it less than a week ago! I think you have made a case that the Internet is capable of great good--it brings people together in love and sharing like no other medium.

I wish you all the strength and peace in the world, and I wish it with all my heart. You are making beautiful marks on the sand of this world with your living and your dying.

The sky is so intense a shade of blue that it brings tears to my eyes to look at it, and the wind tastes of fresh dirt and new green things. The birds are twittering, screeching, squawking, chirruping, and tweeting and the squirrels have been rolling around in the new grass. Pretty soon the college students will be rolling around in the new grass, too--everybody answers the call of springtime! Wherever you go, blue skies and growing things and all the bursting-out joy of God's creatures will be with you.

Sarah Morehouse

Sarah Morehouse <ssm2491@siena.edu>
Poughkeepsie/Loudonville, NY USA - Saturday, April 10, 1999 at 09:55:08 (EDT)

DEAR JAMIE,

I am wandering about in my garden, looking for new green things poking their way up to greet the spring. There, like an old friend, are the tulip bulbs which you gave us for a wedding present seventeen years ago. Its funny, the ones that I put in a proper bed, with bone meal and fertilizer, have long since gone. The ones that continue to put a smile on my face are growing in unexpected and delightful places (where no tulip should ever be able to grow!). There are some growing amid the ferns in wet, acid, clay soil, and another batch that force their way up through the spines of the wild roses.

I feel so helpless, wishing there was something more I could do for you now. All I can think of is to say thank you, for unexpected and delightful surprises all done with a smile and a wonderful impish twinkle in your eye, for your courage and inspiration, for your wonderful support and the hope you gave to me and Buz. I shall miss our circles bumping into each other as they have for the past twenty years.

   Wishing you a peaceful journey to the other side.

   Until we meet again, with love and admiration, Linda

Linda Tripp <Oceanp@midcoast.com>
Tenants Harbor, USA - Saturday, April 10, 1999 at 10:47:14 (EDT)

Dear Jamie,

   I don't seem to be able to get past this desk without another read from your daily letters. Some have had an effect on me far more than I like to admit. They have brought me to tears, taken me to laughter and many places I have forgotten. Paths taken and paths not over time and heart. Your life is a wonderful reminder of BIG heart, and thank you for letting me be part of it.

   Love, Michael (Stevie and Farley)

Mike Mesko <fm@foxislands.net>
Vinalhaven, Me USA - Saturday, April 10, 1999 at 12:31:43 (EDT)

Jamien and friends and family,

   i think of you all often. i think of how blessed i am to live in a community that has lent itself, and has included you all. it absolutely marvels me and reaffirms my belief in man and in the gifts of the world. i don't know you well, i have always enjoyed our brief exchanges. i enjoy your hats, and watching you and philip with the boys. i thought of you often when i was pregnant with isaac, and reminded myself that, yes, life will go on if we have twins and our total of family is six (actually nine with step-children), yes i could have cooked for six. i thought of you today, jamie; i need some advice. i now think of things to do with old sweaters, and even old hats, and we all know what to do with old socks, but what of old mittens? so many colorful, long-forgotten and lonely mittens. any ideas? i love your ideas. renaissance woman, is that the term? a new age renaissance woman. thinking of you and your blessings; with our blessings.

    love, the salas family

cil kinast salas <salseven@midcoast.com>
camden, me USA - Saturday, April 10, 1999 at 14:54:50 (EDT)

Dear Philip,

    I have been following you all from afar these few years. We share children the same age. We often pass one another on Beauchamp Point; I see you with your older sons, during our early morning exercise routines. My thoughts are often with your family.

    I lost my mother to breast cancer when I was fourteen. It is still a loss I have never recovered from, nor ever will totally. I have found having my own child gives me a way to recapture what I had with my mother. It has restored a dimension to my soul that I find so rewarding to have back.

    I would like to offer any assistance for the children, if it would be helpful, discussing my experience. May you find the strength and peace you need to allow this process to carry through...

paiget4059@aol.com
camden, me Saturday april 10, 1999 at 18:42:30 (EDT)

DEAR JAMIE,

Thank you for allowing Jeannie and me to come visit and share a beautiful afternoon with you. It is a time that we will both hold dear for many reasons. I told you at the time that you were truly bigger than life and this Web page is testimony to the lives that you have touched.

I have a great memory of discovering you in the ladies room as we nursed our babies at Alison's wedding so many years ago. Such a moment in time to find ourselves as grownups after only knowing each other as college students in search of….who knew?

The annual Spring Tea has become such a meaningful part of my life and the lives of those who have shared it. Thank you for that wonderful concept that will live on beyond even your imagination. Our thoughts and prayers are with you.

Love, Betsy

Betsy Sessions <betsysessions@usa.net>
New Hartford, CT USA - Saturday, April 10, 1999 at 20:35:52 (EDT)

April 11
• • • •

Today was a great Maine kind of day, the air sharp as a talon, the sun blinding white, and the sky a cerulean marble of blue without even a hint of a cloud. A purple finch practiced its spring song from the top of the white cedar in the yard, lengthening out its phrases and seeming to take pleasure in its voice. We took up the duck boards outside on the walkway and put them away for the year, tempting mud season to make a late and nasty show for itself. And we dug two holes to plant the twin star magnolias that appeared at the foot of the porch with a note sweeter than a bird song, its flowers welling up like an underground stream about to burst into sight. For this suspended moment on this most beautiful of all days, all is here around us….

Tim after returning from California, 1995

Dear Jamien and Philip,

    This is the first time I have visited your Web site. I am so touched by its beauty and lovely thoughts. I think of you every day and send prayers and love. I have just returned from the Odyssey of the Mind State Championship [an academic event]. The closing ceremony took place in the Maine Center for the Arts, which was jam-packed--not an empty seat in the entire place. As they were announcing the Division 1 winners, I had an inclination that Jamie and Micah's team might win first place. I had the pleasure of watching their skit at the Regionals. It was terrific and very clever!! As they announced the third place, I held my breath, Rockport Elementary was not called. Then they announced the second place and again their team wasn't called. Then (to contain the suspense in the air) they handed out a whole bunch of other prizes. Finally, they announced the first-place winners. The twins' team had WON the State and were off to the World! Everyone in our region jumped out of their seats and shouted for joy…You should have heard the applause!! We were all so excited. The kids ran up on stage and then, skipping and jumping for joy, received their individual "gold" medals and HUGE, triple-decker trophy!! I had tears in my eyes. It was all so perfect and a wonderful gift to you both. Your boys are the BEST!! You are the BEST!!

    Sending lots and lots of love to you, Betsy

Betsy Ralston <ralston@midcoast.com>
Rockport, ME USA - Sunday, April 11, 1999 at 00:13:58 (EDT)

Dear Jamien,

    I just learned of your Web site today from Loring Starr. You have been on my mind and in my heart a great deal in these last few days. In my prayers and meditation I have been sending you healing. In the last week, each time, I have experienced you as emanating a kind of golden light, shimmering and peaceful, strong, yet filled with love. Reading your Web site today, I see that I have not been imagining things. At Middlebury this summer, I told you that I could see your beauty shining through. You have a beautiful light, and it's clear that it has touched so many people. And even as your illness diminishes your physical energy, it is making your light more powerful.

   I send you my love and will pray that each day finds you in comfort and uplifted by the love of your friends and family around you.

   Robert Buxbaum

Robert Buxbaum <Rbuxfree@aol.com>
N.Y., N.Y. USA - Sunday, April 11, 1999 at 00:59:30 (EDT)

HEY, TIM CONKLING,

   Do you remember me? Of course you do, silly boy. I'm your dear old friend from California, you know, the one who convinced you to dye a big red streak through your bangs. Well, it's been awhile hasn't it? At least a few years.

   When my dad gave me the notice from "www.jamien.com," I instantly felt a deep regret for not having kept up with you and your family. I owe some of my most memorable childhood experiences to you guys. One that sticks out most in my mind was that little detective club that you and your brothers set up. Jamie bought you guys a detective kit complete with "Conkling Brothers" business cards. I was so envious of that club that I'd do anything to belong in it...even if it meant breaking my neck to climb up that huge tree behind your house. I know this sounds really typical, but sometimes I wish I could revisit those days, and I bet you do, too. When I never had to worry about a test the next day or whether or not I'll get into college next year or what I looked like. When I didn't have to drive

100 miles to have fun; everything was right around the corner. I guess what I'm trying to get at is this: those childhood memories were so innocent--we never had to worry too much about whether our moms were always going to be there or not. It was just a given, you know? And I can't imagine growing up thinking anything else...it takes a brave soul to do that, and I have nothing but total reverence towards you and your family.

I'll be thinking about you guys...

Hana Hamilton <Hana146982@aol.com>
Aptos, CA USA - Sunday, April 11, 1999 at 02:34:20 (EDT)

DEAR JAMIE,

As I write this, I sit beneath your print of a maiden being attacked by a dragon. Roses surround her and she bows her head--in resignation? Is that you? I remember you planting flower bulbs by Hadley at Middlebury in the spring. The hope and joy in the endless circle of life.

And I read your tea letter on this remarkable Web site. I felt a kindred spirit. Truly there is a web of spirit that surrounds our world and can be touched, reached, when the will is there. But you must have known that. My prayers are with you.

Ginny

Ginny (Lambe) Guaraldi <vguarald@valinor.com>
Londonderry, NH USA - Sunday, April 11, 1999 at 09:36:50 (EDT)

DEAR JAMIE,

I hope the sun is shining over Maple Street today and you are out again on the deck of your ship. I am thinking of you now, as I have many times each day over the past few weeks.

Probably most vivid among my memories of you was the ferry trip to Vinalhaven on the morning of your wedding and the flags flying in front of your parents' house. At first I couldn't tell what was happening and then all I could see was the flags, and then as we got closer, it appeared that little tiny people were waving them and running with them. It was a spectacular sight and a moment in time I will never forget. Though the times are few that I have told you, my thoughts and my love and my enormous admiration of your spirit and courage have been with you and are with you now, every day.

Always, Jane

Jane Francisco <JAF104@AOL.com>
Portland, ME USA - Sunday, April 11, 1999 at 15:57:52 (EDT)

Jamie--

This message will require going way, way back into the mists of memory to Shoreham, Vermont, about 1970. We have not been in touch for many, many moons (though I do remember one wonderful story of flags flying at your wedding!)--but every Christmas when we trim our tree, nestled among the treasures is an ornament you made for us before you left Vermont. It's a wooden sun, made, I think, out of two shades of wood, and it has graced our tree and made me think of you each year…so that thread of connection is always there, isn't it? Even when we've lost track of those we've cared about, at one special point each year our lives have converged again and been enriched by the knowing. The beautiful ornament you made for me and Geoff will always be a sweet reminder of our long-ago friendship, and we thank you for that. May you find peace.

Val and Geoff Demong <gdemong@together.net>
Shoreham, VT USA - Sunday, April 11, 1999 at 17:33:15 (EDT)

Dear Jamie,

I received a note today about your cancer and about this Web site. After reading about your tea ceremony and some of the wonderful things you have done with and for so many people, I am impressed by the incredible life you have lived. It's way too soon for you to be off on the next voyage.

I will have tea with my friends this week and share your concept of the ceremony with them. Living on the other coast has kept me distant from much of my family for many years. As the years pass, I find this increasingly difficult as I have not been fortunate enough to have found a partner and created a new family. I've worked for the past ten years on environmental issues in the hope that I will leave the world a better place for my nieces and nephew.

It is truly inspiring to read the messages of your friends. I hope you will be able to enjoy spring flowers from the chair on the deck of your cruise ship.

Kelly Richards, bridesmaid, and Jamien arranging wedding flowers, Rockaway, 1980

Today I photographed tulip fields and if I were up on the technology I'd be able to download images and send you flowers over the Net, but I'm still in the analog mode for photography.

Sallie Sprague <ssprague>
Bellingham, WA USA - Sunday, April 11, 1999 at 18:12:39 (EDT)

Dear Jamien,

   Had tea with you on Monday, at Silvershell Beach, facing, as close as I hope, northeast, Maine, and Rockport. Read a little, thought of you, and remembered your laugh--always lurking at the corners of your mouth and dancing in your eyes. Am pleased I will be able to send you messages at this site. Had my first glimpse of the twins on the Home Page, although by now I know they are a bit taller.

   Know that I keep you always in my heart. My best to you and the extraordinary men in your life who make this possible.

   Zora

zora <zlynch@tabor.pvt.k12.ma.us>
Marion, MA USA - Sunday, April 11, 1999 at 19:33:38 (EDT)

[*Zora Lynch worked with Jamien at the Teacher's Information Exchange in 1981.*]

Dear Jamie,

   You have been so much in my thoughts these days. I have just returned from Japan, where the cherry blossoms were in full, fluttering bloom and the snow was still on Mt. Fugi-san and I had the rare opportunity to savor a quiet cup of "o-cha" tea with you and your many friends from around the world once again--just about sunrise on the sixth in Japan as you were approaching dusk in Maine on the fifth.

   What a wonderful tradition you started! It keeps growing and growing and gives us all such a great chance to be together at a distance, cutting through space and time, to reflect on all the times we've been together face to face, the meals eaten, words spoken, laughs laughed, paths taken. Anyway, I just wanted you to know that I'm thinking of you and sending all of my love to you up there in Maine from NYC,

    xoxo, kathy

Kathy Wilson <ksw2@aol.com>
New York, NY USA - Sunday, April 11, 1999 at 20:31:09 (EDT)
[*Kathy Wilson was a classmate of Jamien's at Middlebury College.*]

DEAR JAMIEN AND PHILIP,

    Sam is quite the man about town. He is THE entertainment ticket. Recently we have been gifted with his amazing juggling and magic skills at three highly visible events: the Camden-Rockport High School National Honor Society talent show; the Youth Arts auction; and the Rockport Library Open House today. He is a charming and talented representative of your family, and so much what you as parents have inspired your children to be. Thank you for who you are, inspiring us as parents and community as your children continue to impact us in their own uniquely exciting and heart-warming ways.

    I send you love, and blessings, and spring smells and smiles.

    Jean Forest

Jean Forest <vanforest@acadia.net>
Rockport, ME USA - Sunday, April 11, 1999 at 22:07:58 (EDT)

April 12
· · · ·

It's been a long day's journey into night, but sleep has finally carried the frail vessel of Jamien's wakefulness off its jagged lee shore.
I know she'll be standing off and on during the long night's watch, looking through the dark and enveloping murk for sea room offshore. It's a hard watch, and the nerves fray before exhaustion finally fills the hold. Darkness, darkness, be my pillow.

DEAR JAMIE,

It's been a while since we have even chatted, but I am thinking of a moment maybe seventeen years ago. The Tranquility Grange in Lincolnville. We each had lost a child by stillbirth. You let me know your pain, and mine cracked open. You cried and I cried; and I think we were standing in the middle of a dance floor. It was a vivid, intimate moment. And ain't that livin'? I have a sense that you have made vivid moments with many souls, that you have lived large.

I will keep thinking of you.
With love to you and Philip, Ben Ellison

Ben Ellison <BenE@BenETech.net>
Camden, ME USA - Monday, April 12, 1999 at 00:40:26 (EDT)

Jamien and Buddy, ca. 1973

HI, JAMIE,

This Web page is so great. It is the next best thing to being there with you. I'm also being educated in the world of computers. When I received the yellow postcard in the mail, I couldn't wait until my son, Derek, got home so I could send you something. Every night I bug him to look at Jamie's Web page. Thank you all for updating it every day for all of us. I think I just may have to learn what this Internet is all about.

I just wanted to let you know my thoughts are always with you, Jamie. Last night I closed my eyes and all sorts of memories came flooding in: Moon Hill, learning to ride my bike, walking to and from school with you, Vinalhaven (it must have been at least forty years ago), SopraBolzano and the infamous trip to Venice with Uli and Louis and Mom. You were always so great to keep up with me and send me your yearly Christmas card.

Thanks, Jamie, for being such a beautiful and special friend.

With all my love, Shelley (Sha)

Shelley McMillan Van Hoesen <DMVANHOESEN@worldnet.att.net>
Evergreen, CO USA - Monday, April 12, 1999 at 00:58:45 (EDT)

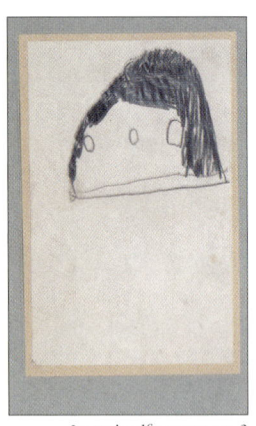

Jamien's self portrait, age 3

Jamie:

 We knew each other in passing at Middlebury and I have read about your many creative and thoughtful projects while you were living on Vinalhaven. I have lived on Deer Isle since 1979 and consider myself a prisoner of Penobscot Bay, imprisoned by its beauty and captured with respect for its power. I know you understand exactly what this feeling is all about.

 Yesterday, I was called as an EMT to the bedside of a neighbor who had died. His daughter said to me about his body, "This is the chrysalis, and by implication the butterfly of the spirit has come forth." What a wonderful image to behold. I am sure your butterfly will be a banner of colors.

 Godspeed

Emily Fuller Hawkins <emmaflea@aol.com>
Deer Isle, ME USA - Monday, April 12, 1999 at 08:53:51 (EDT)

Hi, Jamie,

 I'm so glad that Loring thought to share your Web site address with your Middlebury classmates. It was so wonderful to see you last June, to reconnect however briefly, to see your son who looks so much like you. Whoever is posting the updates has captured the essence of the Maine coast so that I feel that I'm there. Like so many other distant friends who've shared their thoughts already, I sense that my life is going to be changed by reading your words, learning about your tea parties, and hearing how you've lived your life right to the end. Thank you, Jamie. I'll always picture you on Lane's Island, with Penobscot Bay in the background and granite all around. Go in peace.

Franci Vinal Farnsworth <farnswor@middlebury.edu>
Brandon, VT USA - Monday, April 12, 1999 at 09:01:51 (EDT)

JAMIE:

Thank you for the Tea Party and all of the beauty you have brought to our lives in so many ways. You have inspired me and many other people to make our families and communities the center of what is important. I send much love to you and to your family.

Jenny Scheu <redhouse@ime.net>
Portland, ME USA - Monday, April 12, 1999 at 10:36:31 (EDT)

JAMIE--

I so appreciate the creation of this Web site as a non-intrusive way to stay in touch. As one whose heart is always on Vinalhaven, I want you to know that I will take you with me there. Every blue sky day, every low, slanty afternoon light over the harbor, every call of the herring gull, I will absorb and appreciate for you. These blessings of the senses will not go to waste! All of us who know you will bring your spirit to a heightened gratitude for this incredible life that is ours still to inhabit. Rest well, Jamie, I think of you often.

Elizabeth Swain <elizabeth@bartongingold.com>
Pownal, ME USA - Monday, April 12, 1999 at 10:47:17 (EDT)

DEAREST JAMIE:

Many years ago when I left the *Camden Herald*, you talked to me about the future and what it might hold. You gave me great comfort. I wish I could return that kindness in even a small measure. I have thought of you constantly the past few months and was so proud of your son Sam juggling yesterday at the library. You would have been too.

I never saw as much of you as I would have liked, but I always recognized you as one of the wonderful people of the world, which will be a much sorrier place without you. My love to you always.

carolyn marsh <habibi@midcoast.com>
USA - Monday, April 12, 1999 at 15:22:36 (EDT)

Blue Pig, 1978

Hey, Jamie,

    I was out jogging this morning and thinking of all those colorful, bold signs you made for my birthday run a few years back. Like "Smile, you are loved" and "You're halfway there" and twenty or thirty more the specific wording of which I don't recall, although each gave me a huge boost. The one that is absolutely emblazoned on my memory is the one that you tacked up next to a For Sale sign with a mile to go: "If you lived here, you'd be home now!" You know, if I'd had some money on me, I might have made an offer on that house.

    You have given so much to so many so creatively. I know that YOU will always be at home no matter where you are because you'll turn everyone around you into family.

    Love, Bob

Bob MacLaughlin <wordplay@midcoast.com>
Cushing, ME USA - Monday, April 12, 1999 at 16:50:38 (EDT)

Dear, dear Jamien,

    Warm thoughts and energy from the Egg House, where you and Philip started out so long ago. Thank you again for all the energy and advice you provided Betty while she was still alive; she especially enjoyed your special meal in Rockport on the hill at the head of the harbor. And she talked frequently of the different therapies that you shared, and was in awe of the way you were willing to undergo such pain in your treatments.

It's hard to believe that you have been struggling for more than a decade, with tremendous courage and strength, all the while being a mom and a partner, and continuing with all your various jobs and projects. No one has your courage, sparkle, creativity, and good humor.

Thanks also for all you have done for my boys, beginning on Hurricane Island. Langley was over here this weekend searching for the poster you made him with all the artifacts. Remember? How very, very special it was to have you part of that community, and at that time there were not many women! I hope you are at peace now. And when you make the passage please give Betty a hug for me.

Know that you are loved forever. POW

Peter Willauer <pow@mint.net>
Cushing, ME USA - Monday, April 12, 1999 at 18:45:00 (EDT)

Dear Jamien,

Your son, Micah, is in my class. My mom is one of your many friends. Some of my friends and I sold J.M. bracelets to raise money for you. We raised $21.00. Tomorrow I will give this money to Micah for your savings account.

I was one of the many people who sang at your house. We all enjoyed doing this for you and your family. I also enjoyed doing this with my mom.

Hope you are feeling well tonight. You have so many people that love you.

Your friend, Georgia (age 10)

Georgia Smith <seasons@mint.net>
Rockport, Maine USA - Monday, April 12, 1999 at 20:50:15 (EDT)

My dear Jamien,

I last saw you at The Reading Corner. We were all patiently standing in line (more correctly, filling every nook and cranny in the entire store!) waiting for the famous, the charismatic, and the (probably) very tired Brian Jacques to autograph our copies of various Redwall books for our boys. It was quite the community event, I thought. Great to see you and be able to give you a little Reiki while we were visiting. You gave me much in return! I was charged up and inspired, listening to you speak of your commitment to work hard with whatever challenges this cancer brought your way. And you have. Perhaps you have been a teacher for many of us. I know I have felt very lifted in your presence!

I would like to tell just one Jamien story that has a predictably "rippling effect" ending. Jamien, you are always putting into motion these things that grow and grow. Awhile back, in the winter, you told a friend who had some need for energy work that I lived nearby and could help with Reiki. We did do some sessions, and then I found out that she does a special kind of tutoring that was just what my son needed. It grew and grew and she was invited to give a presentation of her type of training to my son's school faculty. Now her work can grow, perhaps more children can get some extra help, my son learns more easily, she gets some healing work done, and an expanded circle of people are touched in a way that helps us all! Thank you, Jamien! This all happened because you brought us together! This is what you have done for so many people.

Here is a spring bouquet of Reiki for you. Close your eyes and just notice the colors of these Reiki blossoms! They are vibrant and full of warmth. Now open your eyes and look to see if there is a fresh flower nearby. Is there? Look deep into it, Jamien. There you are!

Love, Martha

Martha Spruce <mspruce@nqi.net>
Union, ME USA - Monday, April 12, 1999 at 21:53:18 (EDT)

These silk-screened prayer flags made by Antonia Munroe hung over Jamien's bed in her downstairs room.

An intense low-pressure cell over the Canadian Maritimes sagged down over the coast this morning, bringing in a rare "backdoor cold front." Northerly winds whipped and worried at the five Tibetan prayer flags hanging on the clothes line over the porch, until their edges began to slat and fray. Kirsty, the hospice volunteer, who materialized out of the lowery morning gray, took the tattered threads of our lives and helped gently weave them back together. The front finally spent its fury by dark when we too let go for another day.

April 13
• • • •

DEAR JAMIE,

    I have been thinking of you. Every morning after the kids get on the bus, I take my daily hike up Beech Hill. There I sit on my favorite rock. I sit there and think of all the things I am grateful for, I sit and pray, I throw a stick for my furry friend, Baron, sometimes I sing, but mostly I just watch "life" happen. It is beautiful up there. I can see for miles and miles. These are my best mornings, when I can let go of all the daily tasks yet to do and just watch life "happen." It soothes my soul. Today is bright, crisp, and clear. The birds are happy, happy, happy! I will think of you this morning as I sit on my rock. I know you are in a good place…so peaceful…your soul is being soothed by all of this love that surrounds you….it is immense….it is eternal…. so long, Jamie…

Cindy Kava <kava@mint.net>
Rockport, Me USA - Tuesday, April 13, 1999 at 08:48:46 (EDT)

Dear Jamie,

Winnie was with you sipping tea on April 5, out on our old deck in Freeport. When we finally came back to New England in 1995 after twenty-

Jamien and the boys at a Mother's Day picnic, Pleasant Mountain, West Rockport 1995

two years, you answered a note from Winnie with a kind of local benediction that rings in my head all the time: "Maine is a wonderful place for children." I'm always grateful for that small bundle of words because some things spoken resonate, and are never lost again. Our thoughts are with you.

   Our love, Jack Kartez & Winnie Shivelhood-Kartez

Jack Kartez <jackk@usm.maine.edu>
Freeport, ME USA - Tuesday, April 13, 1999 at 11:06:05 (EDT)

DEAR JAIME,

   I've been meaning to write but didn't know what to say…anything I would say would seem inadequate…but if I don't now, when?

   I love you. Carlene

Carlene Michaels c/o Aviva Rahmani <ghostnet@foxislands.net>
Vinalhaven, Me USA - Tuesday, April 13, 1999 at 11:10:34 (EDT)

DEAR JAMIE,

   I overcome my shyness to add to this collection. The modern-day version of carrying a stone to Chartres. A sacred place created on the Internet. I recall watching you stand so straight and be so gracious at the Hat Sale. Every time I was about to whine about how tired I was, I'd look at you and laugh at myself. Thank you for inspiring me to whine less and do more.

   Love to you and yours, Andrea Itkin

Andrea Itkin <andrea@benetech.com>
Camden, Me USA - Tuesday, April 13, 1999 at 11:11:32 (EDT)

Jamie, Micah, Sam, Tucker and Tim
Easter Egg Hunt Maple Street

DEAR JAMIE,

You cannot imagine how I have been affected by the outpouring of love for you so honestly and magnificently revealed on jamien.com. I went for a short walk along a quiet stretch of the Pacific Ocean at dusk yesterday, and thought of you a continent away. With the waves breaking and the energy flowing back out to sea, it struck me that despite the vast distances imposed by time and geography, none of us are ultimately so very far removed from one another. The life you live--full, honest, joyous--is a model for all of us, if only the rest of us could take the time to embrace life as you have. We've not kept in touch over the years, though from time to time I've gotten word of you and the beauty you've created. But even now, I can easily conjure up the vibrant young woman I knew in passing at Middlebury. She seems to me not so very different from the kind, big-hearted, soulful woman you must have become. An inspiration to all of us.

My love to you. Godspeed. Robin Cruise

Robin Cruise <rcruise2@san.rr.com>
San Diego, CA USA - Tuesday, April 13, 1999 at 14:09:01 (EDT)

DEAR JAMIE,

Not a day goes by that we don't think of you and Philip and your "precious cargo" of boys. You have dealt with this devastating illness with pluck and grit and grace and good humor. In doing so you have shown us how to live! I wish I knew a way to make this next passage easier for all of you. I hope you know how many hearts you have touched with your incredible passion for life. Godspeed, dear lady! The loving hands that reach out for you are a haven of comfort and safety and the company you will keep is rich with experience. Make them hats, for I can hardly wait to hear you all laughing once again! With great love to you all, Dyke

Dyke Messler <methree@midcoast.com>
Rockport, ME USA - Tuesday, April 13, 1999 at 15:44:48 (EDT)

Thank you for this wondrous Web site. I could only think, how appropriate!

>   radiant webweaver, you
>   spiderwoman warrior
>   with silken strands--threads
>   of tensile strength
>   you caught us, all
>   shimmering
>   connected
>   thinking of you - thinking of you,
>   Christie

Christie Hoagland <hoagland@midcoast.com>
Rockport, ME USA - Tuesday, April 13, 1999 at 16:41:35 (EDT)

Dearest Jamie, Philip, and Conkling-Crew!

    I will always remember this as the year I had the spring tea twice! I always serve tea on an early day of spring, you see, inviting friends, children, even a few errant squirrels if I must. Actually, invitations are rarely necessary, as my Florida friends, like women everywhere, call and remind me of my duty, if I seem to forget. "It's spring," they say, "time for tea!" And we always praise Jamie's brilliance and wisdom: what a grand idea to come together and chat, to be open to one another. I recall that long-ago first message, complete with tea-bags! "Ease at least some of the world's misery."

    I bless you, Jamie, for making a difference in my life, so many lives, every year, forever. My prayers are with you, as they have ever been.

   Always--Bridget

Bridget Balthrop Morton <bridgetbal@aolcom>
Melbourne, FL USA - Tuesday, April 13, 1999 at 17:30:23 (EDT)

Dear Jamie,

   Today I read some of the entries in your guestbook and something inside me moved. I did not think words on a screen could be so powerful. Jamie, the way you live your life has taught many of us that we can live much more fully, much more deeply, much more directedly. Thank you so much for living true to your own heart and for choosing not to ignore your intuition. You have made a huge difference in this world. You are an inspiration.

   All love to you, Liz Soloway

Liz Soloway <bsnider@erols.com>
Washington DC, USA - Tuesday, April 13, 1999 at 22:24:59 (EDT)

Dear Philip, Tim, Sam, James, and Micah,

   Congratulations, first off, to James and Micah for doing us proud at the OM [Odyssey of the Mind] competition. I hope your mom knows what a great job you did announcing this and displaying your medals to us all at church. We were all very puffed up and felt privileged to be in the company of such distinguished celebrities.

   Thank you all for what you are doing for us all by communicating to your mother/wife our thoughts, and for sharing yours with us. We are all keeping the vigil with you. I wish I could hold your hands, but I really am, you know.

   Much love, Sue and Ken

Sue Crane <craneski@midcoast.com>
Rockland, Me. USA - Tuesday, April 13, 1999 at 22:35:21 (EDT)

By noon today the porch was filled with flowers in front of the chalkboard covered with kind words and notes clipped to the door. On the counter inside, plates of cookies materialized, one of them decorated with a mussel shell filled with lavender and cobalt beach glass polished by the tumbling rote, and graced in the center with a gray stone in the shape of a wave-worn heart. In the afternoon, FedEx brought Carolyn Brady's watercolor of a teacup with a piece of brownie on the edge of the saucer. How can all these joys and sadnesses be encompassed by the sentient world? Words fail us all at times like these; and in the end, words simply become whispers, and whispers become the breath of the wind carried aloft on wings.

April 14
• • • •

Dear Jamien,

Just like the daily prayer routine in a cloister, every morning and evening I log onto my computer to join the circle of prayerful attendants who surround you with love and admiration for a life lived with spontaneity and spunk. Thank you to those who keep us posted of the day's events as well.

I'm remembering your presence for the Hats Extravaganza this January, sitting gracefully at the entrance table greeting everyone with hi's and hugs, proudly wearing a Flea Circus creation--the one I liked best was the hat with the red bird on top with the tail feathers that bobbed up and down. When I was writing the press release for the event and trying to capture its spirit, you summed it up: "It's a hoot." Reading the memories from your many friends and family all over the world, I am struck that you have approached your living with that same sense of humor in the face of the pain and suffering. You were concerned about the environment, yet found fanciful and fun ways to address some of the issues of wasting the earth. Blessings on you and your family. Love, Andy

Andy Burt <adburt@wiscasset.net>
Edgecomb, ME USA - Wednesday, April 14, 1999 at 07:05:50 (EDT)

Dear Jamien,

As I took the dogs for a walk early today I thought of you as I do every morning. Many of our friends are back to herald in the spring. The Great Horned Owl returned to the forest last night and was a solitary voice at 3:00 this morning. The pair of ospreys that nest in front of the house are back and did their high-pitched song outside the window at 5:00. The little flycatcher who nests in the shed each year has also returned. She beats with her wings on my bedroom window every morning to remind me of her presence.

I hope your night was restful. We send you and the boys our love and a little touch of spring.
 Love, Katie

Katie Bauer <kbauer@mint.net>
Rockport, ME USA - Wednesday, April 14, 1999 at 07:16:48 (EDT)

Dear Jamien,

You and your wonderful men are always in our thoughts and prayers. Just a note to share with you how absolutely wonderful Sam was at the board of selectmen's meeting last week. Several of "our boys," and some tired parents, waited two long, tedious hours to ask the selectmen to pay the insurance for the Teen Center to enable skateboarding to continue.

Sam was, of course, the only one courageous enough to speak, and he, with great poise, read a letter they'd written. He so impressed the selectmen that they agreed to try and find some money--a breakthrough that has generated (relatively) positive press in the *Camden Herald* and *Ligature*. You have given Sam great gifts of grace under pressure and the courage of his convictions. We feel so lucky Ned has him as a good friend.

I miss sharing our parenting, skateboarding, snowboarding discussions at the Bagel Cafe, and particularly the wit and wisdom you share on all these issues more than you can imagine. Please know that we're all looking out for "our boys" always.

Neale, Ned, and Nellie join me in lots of love, Betsy

Betsy Perry <sweetfam@midcoast.com>
Camden, Me USA - Wednesday, April 14, 1999 at 07:23:02 (EDT)

Dear Jamie,

Cynthia told me about the Web site last night as we sat drinking tea and catching up. I have always thought of you as a friend and admired you! And I have my mementos. The book you wrote, *Classroom Cooking*, was my bible back in my teaching days and I still can't part with it!!! I used that little book all the time to find inspiration for my own ideas!

And I have a beautiful, large, green fish hanging in my living room--a European trout! It's one of my most treasured possessions! Please know, that as you set sail towards the healing warmth of the light, all of us you have touched are with you and we will meet again! Godspeed, Jamie. Love to you and your family and friends, Pam

Pam Alley <pambyall@foxislands.com>
Vinalhaven, ME USA - Wednesday, April 14, 1999 at 10:28:43 (EDT)

Fish Pennant 1979

Good morning, Jamie,

We met last night at Ruth's house…We all enjoyed our special time together. It reminded us of a wonderful winter day when you brought all your bits and bobs, stamps and glitter sticks, and guided us through the sticky art of collage. We made Valentines for our sweethearts and members not able to attend. The cards were beautiful. You brought out the best in us.

We all have fond memories of that afternoon with you and all the fascinating and funny adventures you have shared with us over our years together. You, Jamie, are our Queen of Hearts and always will be! Everyone is holding you in her thoughts and prayers. We love you.

The women of the Midcoast Breast Cancer Support Group

The women of the Midcoast Breast Cancer Support Group Knox County, ME USA - <humm@midcoast.com>
Wednesday, April 14, 1999 at 10:47:31 (EDT)

Dearest Jamien,

Sitting here at my desk, I have the most wonderful view of Carver's Harbor and the Lane's Island bridge. The Creek is tranquil and the birds are dancing through the air. Your spirit is so alive here.

Thank you for your many kindnesses and helpful tips when my twins were born. Our interactions were few, but I've always felt a special bond with you. You're one of those special people who always has a twinkle in her eye and glows of happiness.

One of my favorite memories of you comes from an incident that took place a couple of summers ago. Alex and Libby decided they needed a little cash for something and set up a cookie, iced tea, and "precious items" table in front of our house. Some time afterward you and your boys drove by and gave us a big wave as you headed home. Well, it wasn't ten minutes later that the three of you were right back with money in hand, ready to buy some goodies. After purchasing soggy cookies, warm tea, and some ridiculous video on money-making tips, you took a picture of your twins and mine. It is such a sweet photograph, and a moment I will always remember and cherish. Thank you.

    Until we meet again, Jamie, may God hold you in the palm of his hand.

    Love and blessings, Kris, Steve, Alex, Libby, and Matt Young

Kris Young <icreek@foxislands.net>
Vinalhaven, ME USA - Wednesday, April 14, 1999 at 14:58:20 (EDT)

Jamie,

    I take the invitation literally, that one may write even if a personal knowing and friendship is remote. I met you only once: at the Island Schools Conference held at the Seacoast Mission in the early 1990s. You offered an exhilarating workshop on art and education. I didn't know who you were and remained one of those in the audience, impersonal, yet deeply moved by what you had to say.

    For a long time I've wanted to say thank you, aware how inhibited and shy I can be at extending what is honestly felt toward another. So as temporal time moves on and as you move on towards, I suspect, higher purposes, I finally would like to say thank you!

    With gratitude, Tony Burkart

Tony Burkart <burkart@acadia.net>
Franklin, Me USA - Wednesday, April 14, 1999 at 15:23:31 (EDT)
[Tony Burkart was Missionary Pastor of the Maine Seacoast Mission from 1983 to 1992.]

Family Christmas card, 1989

Dear Jamie,

Thank you for the many times you have helped to enrich this world through careful thought and reminders that as custodians we have options and should explore them. Jamie, you are a star. I can see your newest banner: Jamien-- Milliner to the Angels. I know my mother will want one!

Love to all, Dorrie

Dorrie Getchell <torngat@tidewater.net>
Appleton, ME USA - Wednesday, April 14, 1999 at 16:19:47 (EDT)

Dear Jamie,

I recall the first day that I met you. I think it was in 1983, maybe 1982. I had received a phone call from a new acquaintance, someone I had not yet actually met, but who would grow to become my best friend. She asked if I would come and meet her, but if I didn't mind, could I first stop by Jamien's house on Vinalhaven and pick up her children?

I will never forget that image, a great white house, with a driveway ending in an area with a small yard. The yard was filled with beautiful children, none of whom I knew, all of whom I came to know, and they were all filled with joy, love, and happiness. In the center was you.

As I think back now, they were all like little angels. You, in the center, were in love with the very scene, the very moment. You have always been that image for me--a tower of love and happiness in the midst of angels. Perhaps, as you journey to the next place, you will find yourself in eternity amongst these angels. With our friend Christine. And with Christine's last words describing the place where you will find her, Betty, and your loved ones now and forever, "It's beautiful." You are so loved.

Victoria

Victoria Woodhull <RLEJ06A@prodigy.com>
Cushing, ME USA - Wednesday, April 14, 1999 at 20:01:55 (EDT)

[Christine Stephenson, Jamien's good friend and a fellow mom, died of cancer in 1989, at the age of thirty-six. Betty Willauer is mentioned several times in this collection. Her own death from cancer preceded Jamien's by three months.]

JAMIEN, PHILIP, TIM, SAM, JAMIE, AND MICAH,

I am forever thinking of you all. Vinalhaven is forever changed for me since you have graced it with your presence.

Jamien, a beautiful and gentle journey to you; it is an immensely powerful one for us all. The stars have shone brighter for me since I met you. Your incredible spirit is ever present in my life and in so many others. I always will be inspired by your journey. If only I could have known more of it.

I regret my note is simple, but I cannot find the words that give justice to the immense feelings that penetrate deep into my aching heart. If only I were on your side of the country; I wait restlessly for summer to show its face. A bird in flight is a beautiful thing.

Much love to a family so full of light, Lenora

Lenora Ditzler <lditz@urbanschool.org>
San Francisco, CA USA - Wednesday, April 14, 1999 at 20:13:17 (EDT)

Dear Jamie,

Just had dinner with Alison Parker (Middlebury '74) and her husband. She told me of your long struggle with cancer and of this Web site. I came directly home to find you. Have thought about you much over the years.

I remember many things about your indomitable spirit and about the project we did for David Bumbeck's design class. Yours was handed in a week late but it was so magnificent that he forgave you everything. You had created a pieced quilt for the project--had followed all the requirements but come up with something unique and completely unexpected. I remember being terribly impressed at the time.

Many years later, after graduate school and two sons, I started a quilting business here in Middlebury and ran it for a number of years. It feels like I have lived a number of lifetimes since I saw you last--some swell and lovely and a couple that I would not wish on anyone. Sometimes at night I go to sleep surrounded by an endless array of the most exquisite textile patterns ever made. Perhaps your next life will look something like that and I will meet you there. Rest well.

Fond regards, Christine Fraioli, Middlebury '74

Christine Fraioli <fraiolovt@aol.com>
Middlebury, Vt USA - Wednesday, April 14, 1999 at 20:48:47 (EDT)

Dear Jamie,

Few purchases have been as satisfying as my "Jamie trout" and my "Jamie hat." I'm not a great shopper, but I knew instantly when I saw the trout on

North Haven and then later THE hat that I wanted to own them. I wanted them because they were made by your hands, with your mind and heart, and I knew I would treasure them and I do. Every chance meeting, every conversation with you, Jamie, has been in-the-moment, poignant, in-the-eyes. I'm sending you and your men my best love and hope. You're the best.

Deb Meehan <maplesyrup@midcoast.com>
Camden, ME USA - Wednesday, April 14, 1999 at 21:13:41 (EDT)

   I am a friend of Susan Katona's and lost a close friend to cancer about a year ago. I have just taken a little time to see this incredible thing you have started and stand amazed at the awareness, love, perception, and deep thoughtfulness that can flow over these airways, if in fact that is what they are. It is truly an inspiration and I thank you.

Lynn Osborn <archlynn@aol.com>
Brookline, MA USA - Wednesday, April 14, 1999 at 21:30:02 (EDT)

April 15

April storms have lurked for most of this week somewhere to the east, wrapping us all in their raw, gray bedclothes while we wait to exhale. Spring never comes easily to the North, and now it seems ever more reluctant to flee the late grasp of a dying season.

   Weathermen are like doctors and nurses; they come and go and do their best to describe the effects of occluded fronts, atmospheric disturbances, and troughs of low pressure, but ultimately they cannot say what tomorrow will bring. We gather in small knots outside Jamien's small room whispering the hours away. In the end, we don't need a weatherman to know that the raw winds that seep in the bones will blow from the north and east.

Dearest Jamien, Philip (my dear and strong brother),
Tim, Sam, Micah, and Jamie,

How is it that the sun can shine, that the birds can sing, that the smell of the earth can be so rich, that the flowers can push out of the hard soil and gloriously move in the breeze, and all is not right with this world? I do remember the first time I met you, Jamie, as my sister-in-law to be, so loving, so vibrant, so beautiful, so generous with your heart. And over the years, the four most beautiful boys anyone could ever hope to have. I know you know we hold them and Philip so dear to our hearts and will forever. They will always be so well-loved. Seeing you at Easter meant so much to me. Thank you for your precious time and love.

Melissa Winstanley <MWinstanly@aol.com>
Wellesley, MA USA - Thursday, April 15, 1999 at 09:37:18 (EDT)

Dear Jamien and family,

Tea has been one of my anchors for some months now since my husband and I uprooted our otherwise satisfactory lives and followed our dreams home to Vinalhaven. I have been joyous to discover how deeply the ritual of tea time was already engrained into the fabric of Vinalhaven life. I was invited by a friend to join your tea on April 5. Since that day I find myself continually reflecting on the energy unleashed by your love and your legacy. Philip, Lee, Dick, and the boys, please let us all know in the days, months, and years to come if there is any way we can help use this fabulous energy and network of friends and all of our love to help any of yours and Jamie's quests in any way!! Thank you for your legacy and your inspiration. Have a glorious journey.

May peace be with you all, Kathy

Kathy Warren <kwarren@vhaven.sad8.k12.me.us>
Vinalhaven, Me USA - Thursday, April 15, 1999 at 10:25:45 (EDT)

A very dear friend of mine told me about you and your family. I have read your Web page and wept. To be loved as much as you are is quite an accomplishment. You have touched the lives of so many. In this difficult time for you and your family, I would like you to know that you have made an impression in my heart that will last a lifetime.

May you all find peace and happiness in the days to come.

God Bless, Rosie

Rosie
Newburgh, NY USA - Thursday, April 15, 1999 at 12:07:34 (EDT)

Baby quilt for Nina Harris, neice

HI, JAMIE,

I was drawing a sunflower today, appreciating the way drawing something makes you notice what matters--and it occurred to me that that's what you do, too.

Love, Jeri

Jeri Hamlen <mhamlen@mediaone.net>
USA - Thursday, April 15, 1999 at 16:09:28 (EDT)

PHILIP--

I hang every night over this flickering window like a frigate bird soaring and watching for some sign below. Words fail me. I think of you and of Jamie and of the boys all in their respective cradles of emotion--wondering what you are going through and wishing there was some magical thing that I could say to still the roaring waters, ease the pain. Kathy sits with me and scrolls and wonders and queries of this family that she's heard so much of and knows only so recently. We see Jamie on the rolling teak deckchair in the sunny lee, blanket pulled high and a favorite hat perched like a sea bird--a lighted smile splitting the springtime airs, blue on high overhead, surrounded by a loving throng, passage-bearer, outward bound. What can we do? What can we say?

Jamien, dear--Godspeed from ole' Billy Bones--I will set a watch for you in the fair weather skies…

love to all

Billy Schwicker <bschwicker@aol.com>
Ramrod Key, FL USA - Thursday, April 15, 1999 at 18:07:46 (EDT)

DEAREST JAMIEN,

One of my favorite stories of yours concerned the time when you were starting as the Recycling Queen of Camden-Rockport. The twins were tiny, Tim and Sam under ten, and yet all were fully educated to the importance of "use it up, wear it out, make it do or do without." You were in your van, with all four boys, in Boston. Driving along you passed a dumpster on which you saw, sadly, a deceased cat. Not wanting to upset the boys you tried to draw their attention to the other side of the harbor, but Sam, at least, would not be fooled, and with a cry of indignation he exclaimed "LOOK at THAT, the waste of a perfectly good cat!"

Like all others, I never remember an encounter with you that wasn't clear, intense, humor-filled, creative, and memorable. You have spread all your courage so lavishly, that each of us has at least a tiny piece to use as "starter" to make more, let it rise in a warm place, bake it in the fires of experience and love, and then pass it on to nourish others, as you have so extravagantly nourished us--and continue to nourish us. With dearest love, you will always be with us on Hurricane, on Vinalhaven, at the UU church, in Rockport, in humor, in light, in every creative moment.

Thank you, Susan

Susan St. John <susan@midcoast.com>
Owl's Head, ME USA - Thursday, April 15, 1999 at 20:11:32 (EDT)

This morning broke clear-eyed, not even red-rimmed; a thing of beauty wedged between intense storm systems. We were awakened by a robin who had a lot to say for itself, and although it may seem ungracious, the silences between its songs were purer than the songs themselves. Jamien told us of being visited, not in a dream, but while she was there and awake. Christine, a friend who died of cancer ten years ago, linked arms with her with a big smile. She has also seen Marcy, her sister, who died a year-and-a-half ago, and Gramma Van Lupine, as she calls her maternal grandmother, although she had to get down close to her face before grandma recognized her. And then a group of midgets on motorbikes. Go figure. Must be a circus out there she can't wait to join.

April 16
• • • •

GOOD MORNING, JAMIEN.

For one who rarely surfs the net, this is an odd and wonderful experience hitting a button and watching you and the tiny twins pop up on my screen. Very fitting as I light my "Virgin de al Caridad del Cobre," my Jamie remembrance candle, for the day's work.

How, Jamien, did we ever get these wonderful boys of ours--each so different and so completely special? Our big boys and our men will be together this weekend--Jed has already hit the road for New York. I'm sure they will all enjoy this.

Love to you, Jane

jane wholey <wholhorne@msn.com>
New Orleans, LA, USA - Friday, April 16, 1999 at 09:36:00 (EDT)

[Jed Horne, Jane's husband and Philip's college roomate, with his seventeen-year-old son would be joining Philip and Tim for a tour of New England colleges over the next several days.]

Dear Jamien,

I've spent a lot of "time" with you these past few days--sharing Micah's and Jamie's excitement and pride in the OM team; Sam's wonderful show at the Rockport Library; and more. Each day as I doggedly worked on creating a new asparagus bed, digging through layers of soil and rock and rock and rock and more rock, I'd think about your love for this precious earth and all the stories you've shared, all the recycling ideas and crafts with our church kids.

I wanted to let you know that on Sunday, May 2, on Micah's and Jamie's birthday, the church school kids will carry out your wish to share May baskets with our immediate church neighbors. The next two Sundays we'll be putting to use many of the wonderful ideas and baskets and other odds-and-ends you shared with us to create joys of spring to share with our neighbors. Your invitation to tea and some teabags will be part of those baskets, too!

With much love, Stevie

Stevie Kumble <skumble@midcoast.com>
Rockport, Me USA - Friday, April 16, 1999 at 19:00:47 (EDT)

I remember the day Jamien was the winner of the turkey shoot up Geesers Field, and outshot every man on Vinalhaven. Your prize was a big white turkey, live, which you took home, dressed out, plucked, and cooked for Thanksgiving dinner. Those were the days, Jamien.

Walter & Lois Day <wlday@foxislands.net>
Vinalhaven, Me USA - Friday, April 16, 1999 at 19:06:31 (EDT)

Hi, Jamie.

I wanted to let you know I'm thinking about you and your family.

I remember clear as a bell the art classes you taught me when I was a child on North Haven. You were my first art teacher. You let us dive into finger paints and really go wild with them. We also made little candles in the small sand box. Mine was a little yellow imprint of my hand. I was so proud. Your hand has touched so many of us--we have all been so lucky to know you.

I'm sure my mom still has that candle up on North Haven.

Take care, Jamie, and be peaceful. All of my love to you and your family.

xo, angela adams

angela adams <rugs@angelaadams.com>
portland, me USA - Friday, April 16, 1999 at 20:02:36 (EDT)

Jamien, Micah and Jamie, 1988

DEAR JAMIE,

I just had a wonderful dinner conversation with my twelve-year-old son, Owen. We were talking about the Egyptian pyramids and were thinking that the beliefs that motivated the Egyptians to build them have changed with history. It is amazing that the knowledge of how the pyramids were built has all but been lost. Thousands of years later we wonder how they really did it.

This way of communicating is like the pyramids in that it is technically complicated but simple people like me can participate in this incredible monument to you. The notes and poems, the flowers delivered to the front door, the art that arrives via FedEx, the jewel-like beach glass and a small, heart-shaped stone are our treasures, which hopefully will ease your journey. These offerings may seem rather ephemeral, but the love they carry to you is more precious than all the treasures of King Tut's tomb.

All good wishes and love, Kate Mahoney

Kate Mahoney <bcphoto@maine.rr.com>
Yarmouth, ME USA - Friday, April 16, 1999 at 20:45:18 (EDT)

Sunday Fun Race, Camden Snow Bowl, 1991

DEAR JAMIE, PHILIP, AND BOYS,

Robin just shared your site with me and I must say what a lovely idea it is. Such a thoughtful way to stay in touch. Though I left Vinalhaven years ago, frequent comments from island friends and family about your good efforts, as well as working with Philip for several years, have made a deep impression on us both.

Spring is unfolding around us here in Stonington, with crocus and green grass spreading over garden and lawn, fading winter's last browns and tans like magic. It reminds me of gentler times growing up on Vinalhaven. And of how you and your family have helped us islanders to keep it that special place it seems. Special thanks for working and sharing with us, from me and us.

Ted

Ted Ames <ames@hypernet.com>
Stonington, ME USA - Friday, April 16, 1999 at 22:49:49 (EDT)

JAMIEN,

I continue to replay the wonderful times I have spent in the company of Tim & Sam. Our time is filled with laughter and insightful conversations. I am constantly in awe of their gifts and the open connection they have to these gifts. I want to thank you for the privilege of sharing the company of your sons.

There is another piece that I want to share with you and that is I am in awe of the healing you have brought to this community. The courage and strength with which you have met your experiences have inspired so many. Myself included. I thank you.

Scott McPherson <scottmc@mint.net>
Camden, ME USA - Friday, April 16, 1999 at 23:25:38 (EDT)

April 17

• • • •

The twins said goodbye to Jamien over their shoulders as they decamped for an adventure to cousins', aunts', and uncles' houses for their school break. For ten year olds, each moment is so rounded and present as they rush off into their future; would that it will ever be so for them. Sam, who juggled his flaming torches outside his mother's room, created streaks of lights across her ceiling like meteors as we listened to the whoosh, whoosh, whoosh of the dancing flames in and out of his hands. Tim and I leave for his first college tour throughout the ivy'd heart of New England while Grandma and Grandpa and a few friends tend Jamien's flickering candle on the hearth.

So long, so long....

DEAR JAMIE,

This morning I stare at the picture of you holding your babies and remember holding my own. Jamie, you have had such courage in living but oh the courage it must take to let go of life, of your babies, and trust the world will care for them as you do.

You have given them the spirit they need and the courage. And Philip's arms are open and loving. Bless you. Bless them.

Love, Andrea

Andrea Itkin <andrea@benetech.net>
Camden, ME USA - Saturday, April 17, 1999 at 08:38:21 (EDT)

JAMIEN...

How glorious that the love you have shared so freely in this life is coming back to warm you and light your way to the next. My loving thoughts are with you and Philip and your family.

Missy Staunton - HIOBS <brillig42@aol.com>
Rockland, ME USA - Saturday, April 17, 1999 at 10:22:24 (EDT)

Sam juggling fire, during a performance in Wilmington, DE, 1999

105

All-American Shirt, 1979, created for her father's birthday

DEAR JAMIE,

   marcia and i are having tea and started talking about watching the royal wedding. do you remember? you spent the night and marcia came over before the sun rose and we made cardboard crowns, even a tiny one for anna who was just a baby. we ate and drank tea and the pictures didn't come out because the film was loaded incorrectly in the camera. it was always such an event when you were around. i know that you will make those midgets on motorcycles laugh.

   love, sara and marcia

marcia kimpton and sara gilfenbaum <kimpton@midcoast.com>
waldoboro, me USA - Saturday, April 17, 1999 at 14:02:20 (EDT)

MY NAME IS JAMIEN TOO I THINK THIS WEB SITE ROCKS THANKS FOR THE INFO

Jamien
USA - Saturday, April 17, 1999 at 16:02:45 (EDT)

DEAR JAMIEN,

   When we (the two Danes next door) were here around Christmas, you listened to our adventure plans about going out West. You stared at the truck and said "In that one...?"

   Well, we went out West, swam in the Pacific--and if you look out the window, it's back! Thoughts to you from Michael & Erik

Michael <mic@ruc.dk>
Rockport, Maine USA - Saturday, April 17, 1999 at 16:40:47 (EDT)

Bless you for creating this beautiful weaving of friends known and unknown--of love.

Nancy Anderson <nca@maine.rr.com>
Falmouth, Me USA - Saturday, April 17, 1999 at 17:00:38 (EDT)

April 18
• • • •

Oh my, in the end words finally fail. We have been planning to leave and not to leave as if spring could be put on hold, but finally we are leaving so Jamien can stage her frail craft at the edge of the coming tide. And what an elegant construction as always--her hull of woven reeds and dried flowers, with a sprits'l rig, tanbark sail, and a banner trailing aloft. There will be a streak in the night sky. Last night she told me wide awake and clear, "I want you to tell Wendy to add a sentence to the letter she will read at my service. Tell her to add: 'It's like hearing a bird sing at night.'" No one can launch the little vessel now but the great making, mothering tide that laps at all of our feet as we struggle to stay and struggle to leave.

DEAR JAMIEN--

You do not know me but I have known of you and your long struggle for some time. A neighbor told me of this Web site. I think of you daily now as your fragile barque seeks safe harbor. I think of you as I garden; as I take a walk to the beach; yes, as I have a cup of tea in the afternoon. You and your family are in my thoughts. It is too early in the season, but still in my mind I send you a teacup filled with pansies of every hue, and when I plant them this spring they will be for you.

Safe voyage, Jamien. Sally

Sally MacVane <smacvane@aol.com>
Port Clyde, ME USA - Sunday, April 18, 1999 at 07:03:35 (EDT)

Details from All- American Shirt 1979

Amongst these songs of love and praise there needs to be a word about Jamien's family. Never has such nurturing, thoughtful, and quite selfless love flowed so freely, night and day. You should all know that Jamien has been spending her waning hours in the most loving of hands and receiving the very best of care. She is comfortable and at ease. Her needs are being met. She is clearheaded. Philip, Tim, Sam, James, and Micah, along with Jamien's wonderful parents and Jamien's light-filled cousin, Wendy, are all contributing with strength, fortitude, and (strangely but necessarily) humor to make this an extraordinary time for an extraordinary person.

   Kirsty

   Kno-Wal-Lin Hospice Volunteer

<Karkow@midcoast.com>
Waldoboro, Me USA - Sunday, April 18, 1999 at 08:00:40 (EDT)

Breast cancer walk, 1994

Hi, Jamien,

Reading all the wonderful and meaningful words and phrases for and about you is SO fantastic! Such treasures for you and your five fellows! You are such a supreme example to all of us.

I just wish I could send you a bouquet of the brilliant wisteria I just walked under--the perfume is incredible, nose-numbing even. From 5,000 miles away, a virtual bouquet is the only option today--but, thank goodness (and maybe Bill Gates!), consider it sent!!

You've taught all of us so much--from recycling fabric and other things to celebrating Great and Small Events with *significant banners.* Your legacy is immense, and so is the gratitude of thousands of us fans in lots of odd parts of the world. (Your recycled gift bags are a huge hit here in downtown Constantinople!)

Forty-nine years ago, when I was the twins' age, breast cancer took my mother. It wasn't a cakewalk after that for my father or my two younger brothers, but we were able to move onward and upward because she had set us on the right track. She hadn't spread her wings as widely as you have, but her children and seven grandchildren--all grateful for her and her wisdom--can attest to the meaningfulness of those early years. You're in my thoughts (and rekindled memories) more than you can imagine.

Courage, friend--to you and all your family. You're Numero Uno in our thoughts right now.

love, Kathy

Kathy Brandes <Wdsworth@aol.com>
Istanbul, Turkey - Sunday, April 18, 1999 at 08:28:05 (EDT)

Good morning Jamie.

i went to sleep thinking about you last night and had a beautiful dream about you. everyone who has known you was gathered on the big beach on

Mullen's Head on North Haven. we were all looking at the stars and the moon and at what a beautiful night it was. you and philip were standing beside one another and you so softly and peacefully said good-bye and let yourself fall into his arms. we all then very quietly walked down to the water and let the waves carry you out. it was so beautiful as the moon shone on you as you drifted off. for a moment you started to drift back toward the shore and before we could react, you were taken far out to sea. the moon and stars were so bright, jamie. it was just beautiful. the sky was the deepest shade of indigo blue and the white waves and your white skin glowed like phosphorescence. we all watched the water and felt very peaceful about your journey. we had such confidence and trust in the sea that we didn't feel threatened or scared for you. just happy that you were in such good hands. that dream will always stay with me and the thoughts of you and your family trusting the sea and moon to care for you. be peaceful, jamie. everyone is in good hands.

   all my love to you all, angela adams

angela adams <rugs@angelaadams.com>
portland, me USA - Sunday, April 18, 1999 at 11:16:39 (EDT)

The Conkling boys at Lane's Island, 1997

Dearest Family of Jamien:

Yesterday I lived in the soul space of what it might be like to continue to live life while one's beloved wife, mother, daughter, friend was making that most mysterious and awesome passage from life to death. So today when I read your update relating your tentative dance as with spring's comings and goings, my entire body and soul responded in empathy. Such a humble gift placed in such a work of art, your lustrous model of meeting death in the twenty-first century.

I'm not surprised that Christine is one of Jamien's escorts into her new radiant life. In gratitude and love that I know not how to give--

Bridget Qualey <Stetson@mint,net>
Camden, Maine USA - Sunday, April 18, 1999 at 14:31:40 (EDT)

Wow! How incredible that one woman could have touched so many lives in one short lifetime! I just found out about your Web site today, and as I looked at the letters from so many people, I wept, and I smiled. How beautiful that one woman has had the opportunity, the strength, and the joy to live such a full life that has blessed so many hearts. The poetry about you from around the world was beautiful. You are so fortunate to be cared for and loved by so many. I wish for you peace and love, and I send you again the reassurance of Christ's love.

I am not a mother, or a wife, only a twenty-three-year-old student trying to figure out my own life. Your courage and powerful life's message should be a lesson to us all. I only hope that I can be as giving to my family as you obviously are to yours. Thank you for your inspiration, yours and your family's.

Peaceful Journey. . .

Tiffany Dell <divadell@earthlink.net>
Bloomington, IN USA - Sunday, April 18, 1999 at 21:59:43 (EDT)

111

Dear Jamien, and yes, all those men folk in your life,

I, also, have not known what to say to you. I keep wracking my brains, "What didn't I say?" It is a thing so big it chokes me...But, lo and behold, at this very moment I am sitting in the office of an old friend in Ithaca, New York. My friend Ann heads up the Ithaca Breast Cancer Alliance, and she herself is a survivor of breast cancer. I have shown her your Web page and have shared my stories of what a magnificent, unbelievable woman you are.

I want to let you in on a little secret.

Do you remember talking with me in the parking lot, waiting for our boys to be done with sailing lessons? Do you remember that I asked you, no bull, what I could REALLY do that would make a difference for you? Do you remember telling me that you would have hard choices to make back in Rockport, that they would be hard to make without the beauty of Vinalhaven to surround you? Do you remember asking me to send you "things of beauty"?

Well, that little kernel stuck and last July or August I started asking other women to join a "things of beauty" club, to pick a day each month as Jamien's day. Needless to say, about twenty women eagerly filled up the calendar. At home, I have the original calendar. I would like to tell you the list right now, but it's at home. Roughly, it's Elaine D. and Elaine C. and Carol P. and Carolyn B. and Sue D. and Annie B. and Rebecca D. and, and, and...

Perhaps you already knew about these fairy ladies, perhaps you caught on long ago. Hopefully you have been inundated with beauty these last few months, as I know you have, by not only these ladies but all of the many, many people you have touched.

Jamien, I love you. You have created a strong sisterhood out here on Vinalhaven that is a great gift to all of us. Thank you.

Damn it, Jamien, I'm sorry to be a whiner, but I will sure miss sharing mom stories with you. I will watch for you in the garden and I'll be sure to plant a perennial that is befitting of your strength and beauty.

    Much love to you and your family, Karen

Karen Jackson
Green's Island, ME USA - Monday, April 19, 1999 at 13:40:18 (EDT)

DEAR JAMIE,

    I want to say that you were one of the people who truly touched me, mostly through your children. They are every one brilliant, dynamic, and involved kids, old beyond their years, however older they will become very soon. They flow from you and Philip, people whom I see as really strong individuals and individualists, who more than anyone else in the family have rejected any sort of conventional lifestyle and done things for yourselves, shaping your life and your family as you have wished it.

    This should after all not be a time for regrets and tears, but a time truly to let you know that people care so much about you. That I care so much. Not having you out there in the world is going to hurt. You are a bright shining sun.

Detail from Two Pigs Going to the River For a Drink, 1977

matt winstanley <smsw5608@oberlin.edu>
oberlin, OH USA - Monday, April 19, 1999 at 20:33:01 (EDT)

Tim as Christmas angel, 1982

Dear Jamien,

    Someone wants us to meet, quickly. Reading your spirit as it has slipped into those you love, I'm more grateful than I can say (hushed here on the edge) for having been given this sighting. Hello forever, wonderful woman.

If You Should Die Before I Do,

I'll come wherever you're praised.
Sit or stand in the back, quietly,
as I came whenever I came
among those you've loved. As any
grateful heart knows not how
to thank a source for song. At least
I knew you enough
to comprehend "gave." If you should die first,
I'll come bare-footed when you
are alone. Don't worry, nothing tasteless
to clutter your grave,
only my dust and petals and pollens
from my beds to sift into yours,
and in this way I might come to hold you,
with the others,
perhaps forever.

    Patricia Ranzoni

Pat Ranzoni <PRanzoni@aol.com>
Bucksport, ME USA - Monday, April 19, 1999 at 22:51:56 (EDT)

April 20

Tim and I are checking in from the land of the future. We have been on a college tour with my college roommate, Jed, and his son, who is Tim's age. We've traversed New England as Tim faces the daunting prospect of figuring out what direction the currents of his life will take him. Sam and the twins are safely ensconced at my sister's house, where they watched the Boston Marathon yesterday and saw the fierce determination of runners and wheelchair spinners burn their passions across the sky, true chariots of fire, the day singed with their honor. Out here in the future, so many fresh faces of earnest achievers in learning communities large and small that Tim will join a short year from now. We feel very far away from home, but check here at this cyber station at the Cabot Science Center and with the angels of the night who glide through the Rockport household on silent winged feet. I know they have created a sanctuary where life's last moments are telescoped out into the universe and kept the hearth safe and warm while we find our way back home.

Posted on Harvard College server, Cambridge, Massachusetts

Good morning, Jamien!

I don't know when Philip and Tim are getting back from their college swing, but wanted to let you know I'm staying close by you in my heart while they're away. I am so amazed and joyful that you all seem to have the trust, joy, and love to let "life go on," letting your young ones, whose set is properly toward the future, step forward with the assurance that you are there beneath them, the groundswell that will always hold them up.

Stories of Sam juggling and addressing the selectmen, Jamie and Micah at the Odyssey of the Mind competition, and now Tim on his college tour, fill my heart with amazement and joy. It is such an extraordinary testament that you are already living out of that in you which is beyond death. And not just you yourself (which one would expect from such an illumined being as you have become), but also, you have managed to pass on this same grace to those you love, so that you can hold each other lightly but dearly, finding that "freedom in unity." Of your many triumphs of love, Jamie, this one is to me the most remarkable and moving.

    Keep on traveling toward the light!

    Much love, Cynthia

Cynthia Bourgeault <treaven@saltspring.com>
Salt Spring Island, BC Canada - Tuesday, April 20, 1999 at 11:38:55 (EDT)

Tim as a Christmas angel, 1983

JAMIEN DEAREST,

    I've been setting up a new exhibition at the museum this past week, on English silver from the eighteenth century. Your glowing Cheshire cat smile shines out at me from the teapots, and I flash on your lovely long artistic fingers wrapped around a gleaming cream pitcher. Imagine all the women who've gathered around these same queer little tea things, gabbing, sharing, planning, solving the world's problems, over the past 300 years or so! We'll share tea again, too, Jamien.

    Until then, may your journey be peaceful and winged with the love of all you've touched.

    Deborah

Deborah Shinn <shinnde@ch.si.edu>
New York, NY USA - Tuesday, April 20, 1999 at 13:07:34 (EDT)

GRACIOUS JAMIEN,

    As you are probably aware, your friends have signed up for time slots around the clock in which they light a candle and spend their time with you. It gives us the chance to join with your spirit and heal the hurt in both of us. I have been spending my time with you going on long walks. We have walked the Georges River highland path, the Rockland breakwater, and this past week found us on the top of Mount Battie, drinking in the morning sun as it shimmered across the harbor. I cherish this time all week; I think of you and wonder where we'll be off to next. You'll be pleased to know the dog is always along for our treks. I struggle to find the words to tell you how deeply I have admired your grace and radiance through your long battle. I've learned so much about the strenth of the human spirit and the powerful healing brought by love. Your light will always shine.

    Sent with a delicate kiss for your forehead,
    Diane Batley

Diane Batley <batley@midcoast.com>
Thomaston, Me USA - Tuesday, April 20, 1999 at 20:12:10 (EDT)

Dear Jamie,
    I finally found this morning in a box in the attic my 1980 *Greater Portland* magazine with you on the cover--arms outstretched to the world, face to the sun full of joy, surrounded by your wonderful banners of moons, waves, and shimmering fish. I remember those years well, as if only yesterday, sitting

117

Seven Years In A Tent

On Tim's sixth birthday, we gave him a tent and he and Sam (age four) promptly spent that night in it and subsequent nights throughout the remainder of that first spring, summer and fall.

That first winter after a string of brutally cold nights, Jamien called the family doctor to ask if they were likely to get sick and if we shouldn't bring them in. But the doctor was upbeat, reminding us that viruses and bacteria can't survive outside in Maine winters.

Ultimately they spent every night for seven years living in a variety of tents on a platform in the backyard. They became equipment testers for both L.L. Bean and Patagonia. One cold, dreary, April morning, when Tim was 13 and Sam was 11, they came in and announced they had spent their last night in a tent. It's hard to know exactly why they came in when they did, because they didn't want to talk about it. When it's over, it's just over.

Jamien in an igloo she built in her front yard with her father where she spent her first night winter camping in 1956 at age five

After the first half year of tent living, Tim and Sam began to wonder what the record might be, at least according to the *Guiness Book of World Records*. Their mother told them that when she was a girl she'd heard of someone who'd spent 12 years sleeping out on her parent's porch in New Hampshire. And with the certainty that only young children have about the span of time, they'd responded, "Twelve years, oh, we could do that!"

119

around your apartment, glasses of wine in hand, sharing our hopes and dreams. You have lived yours well. You are such a bright, creative spirit and you have touched so many peoples' lives in more ways than you will ever know. You will always be in my heart and I love you.

   Susan

Susan White <susan.white@umit.maine.edu>
Winterport, Me USA - Wednesday, April 21, 1999 at 08:41:48 (EDT)

Dear Jamien,

  I remember thinking, after I got married, that you think there is just one wedding. The one with the white dress and the rented tuxedos and the inevitable peculiar Aunt with a big hat…but there are lots of little weddings afterward, too. Lots of moments when you say, "Do I? Yes, I do." Sometimes you say it gladly, sometimes tearfully, sometimes through clenched teeth, sometimes holding a new, wet baby (or two) squalling and beautiful in the sudden air…and sometimes--maybe the most important time--you say "I do" when it really counts. When "til death do us part" has suddenly become the closest, real-est, most obviously inevitable and yet stunningly unexpected part of the vow. DO I? Life asks. And then, when it counts most, hurts the most, is hardest of all, you answer Yes. One more time, yes, I do. Bless you both, Jamien and Philip.

  And much love from

  Kate, Zach, Peter, Ellie, and Woolie

Kate Braestrup <KateO@ime.net>
Thomaston, Me. USA - Wednesday, April 21, 1999 at 17:56:44 (EDT)

Moving from Strength to Strength

. . . .

You have opened so many doors…

light floods in, kind faces appear,

hearts open up, my heart opens up.

Did you plan this?

Is this the last and greatest work in

the portfolio of your loving?

Tino O'Brien April 25, 1999

Meg's Field, 1978

April 22
· · · ·

After a long journey throughout New England we return to touch the ground beneath the hearth of our Maple Street beginnings and ends. Grandpa is raking around the star magnolias newly opened to the sun's advancing charms while Grandma folds the wind-fresh laundry. Outside on the porch of the teahouse, Kirsty, Carol, Barbara, and Dottie sit in deep pools of reflection, undisturbed by the stones fate drops into their stillness.

Inside, Jamien is asleep in the frail arms of her beautiful, purple nightshirt. The journal on the kitchen table, kept by her care-givers, tells of her waking yesterday morning, surprised to be still with us. She says she feels like she is hanging by a slender thread. The boys quickly gather at the foot of her bed as a smile slowly blooms at the corners of her mouth. Our few words and hers are both large and small. To be reunited, however briefly, is like the gift of light and love suspending us in midair as sleep reclaims her now constant companion.

TO JAMIE,

I am thinking about you. I hope you have a fun time up in heaven when you get there because I know that you had a fun time here.

Love, Hillary Gordon [age six]

Camden, Me USA - Thursday, April 22, 1999 at 10:43:31 (EDT)

DEAR JAMIEN,

When my cancer news reached you, your immediate and uplifting response gave me strength and continues its sustaining power. In your note you wrote, "I want you to know, in an odd sort of way cancer is o.k. This is a difficult journey. Take all the love you can fit in your backpack. It will in the end be the force that saves you."

You are an inspiration, you goddess of the love-filled backpack, you magnet for love. My thoughts are with you daily. They are thoughts of your good humor, sharing, caring, giving, your love. You give reality to the best that life is about, that influences so many lives. You shine and shine and shine on. Sleep tonight and wake tomorrow surrounded by the love of your wonderful family and a grateful-for-you world of friends.

For Ann too, Tom

Tom Hopps <annhopps@midcoast.com>
Camden, ME USA - Thursday, April 22, 1999 at 09:30:47 (EDT)

Jamien and Sam, Eagle Island, 1985

DEAR JAMIE,

Like so many others, I am busy with memories of you. I have been remembering our first "session" together. It was when you came to the college [the College of the Atlantic] to lead a flag- and banner-making workshop for the seniors, class of--was it 1985, or so?

I remember the slides from far-flung corners of the world where you had traveled, how in unexpected places you had discovered colorful cloth emblems that lent their beauty and whimsey to everyday life. Then the slides of the grand festival at home, where the community had come together to celebrate itself. Banners with images of lobsters and mussels snapped smartly in the fresh winds of the Fox Islands, turned silver-shingled barns into magical palaces. I could imagine the music and the laughter that accompanied their making, their flying…the happiness that sounded in your voice. Inspired we were, and all hunkered down for a long day and night of making our own flags to carry in our graduation ceremony. You brought so much energy to that session, which was a marathon, with sewing machine lessons, bobbin-winding, yards of vivid rip-stop nylon, tales of travel, community, recipes from Poland, and songs from all over.

Irises, 1981

While we worked to create what became a huge, handsome flag symbolizing human ecology, you offered patient guidance, and as an aside gesture to keep your hands busy, collected scraps and whipped up a little banner with a particularly plucky gecko a-wriggle on it. It graced the window of our natural history museum for many years, while the great flag festooned many a graduation tent. Late that night we made our way back to my house, where we sat around the kitchen table for more conversation--and a bonding that has lasted me all these years despite the fact that we have only actually seen each other once since then.

You were the first person I knew who had twin sons after I did, and our dialogue has been very sustaining to me. I keep, tucked in my tattered old address book, your Xmas card of your four sons, including infants dressed up as angels sporting magnificent pairs of homemade wings. I am still stunned that you could pull that off: have twin babies (to join with your two other small sons), make wings, and, yes, haloes, take photo of four grinning guys in various stages of dental development, make the cards, rim them in gold, and actually send them out with personal messages. Before Xmas. Yes, I will always keep that card to remind me of you, Jamie, and of your passion to live fully, beautifully, with love and humor, committed to family and community, despite the odds.

I will remember also your initiation of the ceremony of having tea with friends at an appointed hour, recognizing that the power of women united is an awesome thing, that it can change the world. As we gather together in virtual time and space around the positive energy that you are and will continue to be, we ARE changing the world, Jamien.

I send my love and gratitude to you, dear friend.
Susan Lerner

Susan Lerner <slerner@ecology.coa.edu>
Bar Harbor, Maine USA - Thursday, April 22, 1999 at 13:54:29 (EDT)

OH DEAR JAMES,

I need to thank you for friendship, inspiration, and guidance. We share the Moon Hill bond. So many terrific memories…sculpting with clay or Lee's homemade playdough on the dining room table (I was inspired by your creativity)…Dollhouses in the playroom…You had the coolest room (thanks for letting me and Marce in). Your kites were beautiful…Butterflies and bullfrogs and muddy P.F. Flyers in the swamp.…I followed you down the sledding trail and you helped me drag my toboggan back up the hill behind your house and Mimno's too…

Company Point, Moomoos, midnight skinny-dipping and phosphorescence…You, the older, wiser teen introduced me to tampons and those wonderful Dunbar boys…In High School, I benefitted from your upperclass experience, you got me to join Y.E.S., made helpful suggestions on how one should dress, and generally made being a freshman easier…

On your return from Poland we saw a movie and walked arm in arm in Central Square, felt that sisterhood is powerful, we could do anything, we were both at crossroads, I felt very close to you, your equal for the first time that night.…

I love you, Jamie; you are with me and will always be an inspiration. Toot

"Toot" Simone Faflick Coble <dacobes@net1plus.com>
Townsend, MA USA - Thursday, April 22, 1999 at 23:09:41 (EDT)

Although we didn't call it that when we were young, we used to gather for vespers at the end of the day, and marked our day's passage with this simple verse:

        "*Now the day is over,*
        night is drawing nigh,
        shadows of the evening
        steal across the sky."

April 23
• • • •

Detail from Silver Moons, ca. 1982

Outside, the wind is restless and the prayer flags are more pale at the end of each day in the unblinking eye of the sun. But inside, quietness has tiptoed into the house. The profusion of flowers--lilies, iris, Queen Anne's lace, and tulips--arrange themselves like infinite sides of a still-life, holding the moment like an inhalation, lest the dust of the universe be disturbed. It's a still life at evening vespers.

The photos here made tears come to my eyes for the joy of friends, of people who make the world a better place with their children, their gardens, and their art. I spent some time last week sharpening my father's old handsaw, and when it cut beautifully I thought about how parents give us a way to deal with the world, that maybe they even put hope and joy in our lives that we can take with us wherever we go. A way to see the beauty in snow falling on the peaks, in the first green shoots out of the dark soil. At times in these last few years when I have felt alone or seen the abyss, I have taken pleasure in some of my memories of our times together. I still do and will continue that. Having tea with you this morning, Jamien.

Daniel Whittet <Dan@tvg2.com>
Telluride, CO USA - Saturday, April 24, 1999 at 12:18:48 (EDT)

I have been invited to a ceremony that I believe is in the Jewish tradition of honoring women in our lives who have made a deep impression on us. There was one space left, and they asked me, a stranger to most of them. We are to bring a candle and a piece of fabric that is sewn together with others. I will bring Jamie into this circle tonight, sharing what pieces I know of how she connects us all so profoundly.

Catharine Scherer <JASHODA@AOL.com>
Spokane, WA USA - Saturday, April 24, 1999 at 19:34:40 (EDT)

Jamien, et al.

Every evening I go to jamien.com to see the update and read the newest messages…it's something I must do before I sleep…it is an exquisite word quilt, a rich fabric of colorful images of love and friendship and community and heart-wrenching sadness and amazing joy and grace. May it always keep you warm and safe, wherever you may be.

Missy Staunton <brillig42@aol.com>
Rockland, ME USA - Saturday, April 24, 1999 at 20:20:15 (EDT)

Dear Conklings,

As deep friends of Sam and the rest of the family, we thought it would be appropriate to send our consolences to all. We realize that these are trying times for everyone involved and would like to pass our feelings of pain.
It is the most pleasurable to have grown, and to continue to grow, as friends and practically family with the Conklings. We would like everyone to know that we are here to help in anyway possible and that we will always be there for you guys.

The pumpkin eaters, Halloween, 1998

I hope everyone takes a moment each night to reflect upon what we have all learned from knowing Jamien, and to pass our prayers along.

Love, the guys

Matt, Ned, + Chris (aged fifteen)

Matt, Ned, and Chris <Locke_4@yahoo.com>
Camden, Me USA - Saturday, April 24, 1999 at 20:37:36 (EDT)

Each night I plug in to this remarkable Web YOU have created--a web trembling with aliveness--and I am beckoned deeper, into thoughts about what is important, timeless, precious in life. Your struggle is helping all of us to love more, to treat life with more reverence. Today I saw the cherry and dogwood blossoms so clearly, heard the call of the sea gulls circling overhead and the shape of the waves lapping in the reservoir in a new way because of you, because of you. While your body disappears into sleep, your spirit is quite busy--for it seems to touch each of us--gently, surprisingly, profoundly, as we go through our days. May your rest bring you peace and may your spirit soar.

With all my love, Robert B.

Robert Buxbaum <rbuxfree@aol.com>
NY, NY USA - Sunday, April 25, 1999 at 01:16:05 (EDT)

April 25 *Jamien, who has always been a fanatic about imaginative school projects, would have loved the scene. We are in a large art studio, drenched in light, surrounded by bits of still life from previous classes. Grandpa is working with James on his Roman architecture project, while Micah is constructing a diorama of the greenhouse effect from moss, lichen, and miniature trees.*

Before the boys can go play, they must complete these projects they chose at the beginning of the school year. Micah has figured a way to use Saran wrap to simulate how carbon dioxide gases trapped in the atmosphere cause climate change. James has drawn an architectural plan of the Roman forum, circus, and basilica. But now he must construct a viaduct to finish the project off. The going is tough. All afternoon he has glued Domino sugar cubes together one by one to create the pedestals, while the blocks for the arch must be tapered to fit. A piece of sandpaper is just the thing to finalize the keystone, and there is our mason, sanding the cube, then wetting his finger and dreamily lifting the piles of sweet white sand to his lips for sustenance.

All afternoon we felt her presence flood through the windows, energizing these projects. Why is it that things so sweet and difficult get all mixed up together?

Fresh Fish Banner, 1986

I have thought of this site as a fast-rushing river in which I can only hope to be carried by the current to get the drift. I can only hope that same current is adequately nourishing and sustaining Jamie's family and close friends at this time of terrible beauty.

It is an exquisite spring here, where I still have crocuses in bloom even as the pulsatillas are flowering, but it's dry, dry, dry. As this site is for me: exquisite and parched by the imminence of death.

I can only remark on your remarkable courage and strength in carrying on your lives with dignity and grace in the face of what must surely be heartbreak. I cannot fathom it. I am left almost speechless with admiration at the entire mystery.

Aviva Rahmani <ghostnets@foxislands.net>
Vinalhaven, Me USA - Sunday, April 25, 1999 at 10:00:49 (EDT)

The small child in me wonders about Jamie's trip.

> Whom are the others she will meet?
> Is it too warm or too cold, or is it truly pure light
> As we want to believe?
> "Will there be time for naps?" the small voice asks.
> And whose toys will she play with?
> Will the porridge be "just right"?

I am so scared and you are so brave.

Perry Gates <syrup@midcoast.com>
Camden, ME USA - Sunday, April 25, 1999 at 13:38:52 (EDT)

DEAR JAMIE,

It's hard to know to whom I am talking. To you, of course, but you have become so much more, have opened so many doors…light floods in, kind faces appear, hearts open up, my heart opens up. Did you plan this? Is this the last and greatest work in the portfolio of your loving?

I imagine I see you with a mock serious face, but a twinkle in your eye, slyly and slowly exiting stage left as our eyes turn now to sparkles of light appearing all around from the recesses of cyberspace and memory. Stories flood forth: portraits of tea and a brownie, of hats that spill laughter, whooshing and flashing fire batons, mothers sharing their doubts and struggles and their deep "I do's." You have opened our hearts, I am in love with each kind soul who cries for you, who takes the boys to play, who sends packages with "things of beauty," who lifts their cup in your honor, who remembers…How can we not love each other?

Tino <Ddude22@aol.com>
Montpelier, Vt USA - Sunday, April 25, 1999 at 15:20:45 (EDT)

130

Jamien with Tim, Sam, and friends dividing the Halloween candy, Rockport, 1995

DEAR JAMIEN,

    I have just become a member of the e-mail world and this is the first Web site I have opened up. It is moving and consoling to read the eloquent entries in the updates. Your vivid images remind me of the juice bottles of colorful paints that you used to make and sell to benefit Peopleplace. There is a place in God's future for you that is filled with wondrous colors and you are just the person to appreciate them. I am glad that spring has come and you are still with us. We all need to remember that each day is a gift. Precious and yet fleeting. God bless you and Philip and your children, always.

    Love, Monica

monica kelly <hypfive@mint.net>
thomaston, me USA - Sunday, April 25, 1999 at 19:50:05 (EDT)

DEAR DEAR JAMIE…

    I just learned of your Web site this very day…I have thought of you so often and have kept you and your family close in thought and prayer.

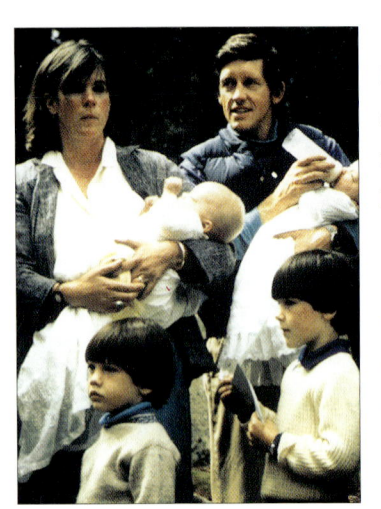

Jamien, Philip, Sam, and Tim with the twins at their christening Hurricane Island, 1988

As I have told you in the past, you first came into our family's life when Fred's mother came to live with us. She first met you in the mastectomy support group. You made such a wonderful impression upon her. Your inspiration made it possible for her to overcome her depression and return to her home in Pennsylvania for four more years of quality living.

You truly are an example for us all…your strength, courage, love of life and what is truly important in life connect you to those of us whom you have touched. We will carry your special touch upon our hearts forever and we are truly made better and the world is truly brighter because you have passed our way. Thank you, dear Jamie, and God bless you and your wonderful family as your life's journey continues.

With love and admiration, Nancy Kneedler

Nancy Kneedler <frenan@earthlink.net>
Rockport, ME USA - Sunday, April 25, 1999 at 20:39:06 (EDT)

DEAR PHILIP,

I thank you for letting us in on a very private process. It has helped us in our own grief. I think so often, too, of Lee and Dick, who have lost their only two daughters so closely together and way before their time. Mary's parents had lost their oldest son four months before Mary's death. Mary was the youngest of five. Bless you all.

Love, Sue

Sue Crane <craneski@midcoast.com>
Rockland, Me USA - Sunday, April 25, 1999 at 22:06:30 (EDT)

April 26
• • • •

A few days ago Jamien floated back to the surface of consciousness and asked, "Why is this taking so long?" Her very good friend and caregiver answered, "Jamien, think of it this way: you are going from strength to strength." This was such a simple and palpable truth that a small smile crept in from the edges of her mouth in spite of herself. So, the body gives out, the voice barely whispers, sight and sound slip away. But Jamien's magnificent, giving heart just knows nothing else.

The heart will have its own way, and thus should it be, that the last flame flickering, long after the last recorded syllable, should be from the innermost chambers of that place in the body where immortal love lies.

Dear Jamie,

Last Wednesday while walking the beach in San Diego, I found access to the Internet at a funky little "organic" coffee house. I put my dollar in the machine and there you were holding your dear twins! It was heartwarming to read all the sections of the Web site and to feel closer to your home in just an instant.

There were two large chairs facing the Pacific Ocean outside on the balcony of the computer room. I envisioned you sitting there (in the purple one with gold dots), so I chose the bright green one next to you. You had a huge smile on your face and we laughed as the breeze blessed us with the sweet scent of the Southern California blossoms. I am thinking of you always.

Love, Barbara

Barbara Baum Freethy <cdsearch@gwi.net>
Brunswick , Me USA - Monday, April 26, 1999 at 14:05:42 (EDT)

Friends are calling friends to say that this might be a good time to light a candle for Jamie. The dear Jamie we all love so much is almost ready to travel on and just as all of our hands holding our warming tea earlier this month focused a deep love in that manner, so might we now collectively shed light on a wondrous strange voyage soon to begin.

Tonight's wind is gently blowing a silvery veil across the moon. It blows from somewhere west of north...it is quietly exhaling down the harbor in Rockport, out across the western bay, over and past Lane's Island...and beyond.

Sweet sleep, Jamie, safe travels, God bless. You are so very loved.

Peter

Peter Ralston   ralston@midcoast.com
Rockport, ME Monday, April 26, 1999 at 20:58:30 (EDT)

April 27
• • • •

The roses of winter still grace the household, drawn and pale; frail yet beautiful in their repose on the sill in their slender vase.

All four boys are finally back under one roof after the twins returned from a wonderful succession of friends' houses. They are finally able to be home because Jamien's hyper-sensitive auditory nerve, a side-effect of her medication, has settled itself down. Hearing, the hospice wisdom has it, is the last sense to desert us, long after sight and touch have departed for parts unknown Micah and James finished their year's projects today at Antonia's studio, which was alternately light and dark under furiously changing skies preceding and following a towering cold front that rolled down out of the Camden Hills. When they returned home, Jamien called them into her room, where they knelt at her bedside. Summoning her breath with an effort like cornering a windstorm, she whispered to them, "You did good work."

Dear Jamien, Philip, Tim, Sam, ,Jamie, and Micah-

Jamien, we were together at Peopleplace with our two sets of twins when my mom was diagnosed with colon cancer. I remember being thankful that you were well and carrying on. I see your bright good face in each of your sons, handsome and smart and now wise beyond their years.

I was with my mother for two weeks taking turns sleeping in the bed so to give my father a break and to be there. I sang to her, I read Phillipians, which was a great comfort. She told me of seeing her grandmother there in the room gently waiting, smiling, loving. She smiled, looking "happily exhausted" at the prospect of "seeing" down a corridor all these students waiting for her to teach them!! Her greatest sadness was when my brother died and she longed all the remaining days of her life to be reunited with him. She told me of being rocked in Jesus's arms. There was a glow about her. It was OK.

I will remember the parties my twins enjoyed with yours at the house, at Walker Park--the bubbles and bikes and huge painted boxes. The banners. Horizons with Kristin and Scouts with the young ones. The sweet note written to me along with the plant when they wanted to join--how could I say no? So my friend, I love you and I cannot say that I am not sad, for I am, but I rejoice and thank God, too, for you and I will always remember.

Love, Heidi, Kristin, Edward, and Elena

Heidi Roggenbauer <Heidi_Roggenbauer.fivetowns.net>
Camden, Me USA - Tuesday, April 27, 1999 at 16:39:17 (EDT)

Micah and Jamie, Camden bike parade, 1990

JAMIE,

A memory came to mind today. Your smile and joy at preparing and presenting a most elegant meal of "chicken divan" prepared on a two-burner in the cockpit of a pulling boat. Somewhere on the coast of the Carolinas, under the moon and bound for the Florida Keys. Thank you. You will always be a gift and a guide.

Steve Bailey <baylore @midcoast.com>
Rockland, ME USA - Tuesday, April 27, 1999 at 19:11:08 (EDT)

Jamien--

I never had the privilege of meeting you, until I came upon your Web site this evening. And now may I say it has been a distinct pleasure and honor to have met you. Jamien, thank you so very much for courageously continuing to teach us all in every blessed moment.

A grateful pupil

Camden, ME USA - Tuesday, April 27, 1999 at 19:12:17 (EDT)

Meg's Field, 1978

Dear Jamie,

What a uplifting experience to read these messages from all corners of the world. The seeds that you have shared with us throughout the years reflect in this Internet garden--a bouquet of friends and family! As I sit this morning in front of my awakening garden, I fondly remember those times we have shared. Fireworks on Lane's Island Beach, early morning breakfasts waiting for the monarch roosting tree to take flight, banners waving from Rockaway to great thankful arrivals on the ferry, blue glass beaches, quarry moms (yes there will be a Zu-Za-Zu band in the parade this Fourth), one incredibly powerful evening last summer, the Zip line, attic crafts, sewing machine engines, and laughs.

Last week, Ladd and I were watching an absolutely brilliant red sunset over the Pacific. The surf had pounded the beach all week, but that night it was soft, peaceful, and we had the entire beach to ourselves. Ladd delighted in finding various treasures for me, having me close my eyes and guess what each was. Placing a cold, wet, flat triangle in my palm, he said, "You think this is glass but it isn't. Remember when we made the blue glass beach?" After several unsuccessful attempts at guessing what I held, he couldn't contain himself any longer: "It's Jamie, Mom--she's with us."

As you continue your journey, we will continue to look for you in ours, beach glass, butterflies, banners, hats, little boys' laughter, groups of women sharing life, children's passionate eyes--yes, Jamie, you will be with us.

    Love, Ang

Angelyn Olson <aolson@foxislands.net>
Vinalhaven , ME USA - Wednesday, April 28, 1999 at 06:57:19 (EDT)

April 28
* * * *

Outside, a cloud floats by the near-full moon like long fingers stroking her hair. Inside, votive candles dance like diva spirits in the corners of her room where Buddha and Ho-Tai sit and wait. The gold-framed icon of Mother Mary, lit by the fiery tongues of angels, glows on the night-table. One by one, the boys part the curtain and sit quietly with these restless spirits as night is drawing nigh.

DEAR JAMIE,

    Years ago, on a very raw, cold, rainy, early spring day, I tucked into Mama and Leenie's for a warm drink. You were sitting there quietly, drinking tea and gazing out the window. You looked to be in some faraway place, a most peaceful expression was on your face. You smiled and said to me, "Isn't it beautiful?" I have thought of that every rainy day since. There are other memories too--Hurricane Island and kids at the Y, but that rainy day is the one I'll carry forever. Thank you for opening my eyes, Jamie. Wishing you comfort and peace.

    Love to you all, Robin

Robin Guist <ghost@mint.net>
Camden, ME USA - Wednesday, April 28, 1999 at 07:49:45 (EDT)

The twins on a windy day at Owls Head, 1997

SWEET JAMIEN AND FAMILY,

I was thinking yesterday about some years ago when Woody and I "borrowed" James and Micah for a day at the beach. It turned out to be a wildly windy day, and we all had to yell to hear one another, but it didn't matter. The boys, brave and curious, stood next to one another at the fringe of the water, spread out their arms, and leaned into the wind...teasing and trusting to see how far they could lean. I thought then, "What great souls...to embrace and lean into, rather than hunker and hide."

I took photos of the boys that day and placed them on the page next to my last editorial...a gift to myself to remember to lean into the wind of whatever comes next.

And Sam, who trusts that he can toss swords, discs, clubs, and can make it look so graceful. Who can even do it all while riding a unicycle. And who once said to me, "I think you should write a story about The Art of Sam." Absolutely.

And Tim...who carries the grace of a wise man and who, one of the first times I met him, offered to help with my computer problems. He was already starting a business, trusting that he had gifts to offer--and was right.

Your spirit, Jamien, infuses each of them. Your boys know beauty because of you. And I imagine that you will always be the wind, inviting them to lean into the strength of you. I'm thinking of you all, wishing you a peaceful journey...With much love and gratitude, Amy

Amy Rawe <amy@hopemag.com>
Brooklin, ME USA - Thursday, April 29, 1999 at 09:37:29 (EDT)

DEAR JAMIEN,

Today my thoughts have been with all of you in diverse and crazy places-- church, Ames, the supermarket. At Shop & Save I was unconsciously drawn to the baking aisle and found delightful cupcake papers to use for the cupcakes we're making to honor Micah's and Jamie's Sunday birthdays and also Tim's May 6 birthday. In Ames, was picking up a few last minute odds and ends for the May baskets the kids will complete Sunday to deliver to our immediate twelve church neighbors--another one of your ideas to spread good will and cheer a little farther.

It's so very comforting every day, my friend, to realize that you're always there. So much of your life lives on in the hearts and souls of those you've touched and even in those complete strangers who will be touched by an act of kindness and gentleness whose seed you planted in someone else's mind. Those precious gifts are endless and will go on and on.

Wishing all of you peace and love, Stevie

Stevie Kumble <skumble@midcoast.com>
Rockport, Me USA - Thursday, April 29, 1999 at 15:49:14 (EDT)

You are loved.

anonymous <same>
same, ME USA - Thursday, April 29, 1999 at 20:40:35 (EDT)

Dear Jamie and family,

I feel as if we are all on this journey together with you…taking lessons…trying to figure out what to do when it is our turn. You have been an inspiration to us all for as long as I can remember and even more so as an adult, mom, and caregiver. And now, you are helping us to find ourselves as you find your path. We will always have you in our hearts and in our spirit. You give us life as you cross to the other side. You are in the songs of all of our hearts. Be at peace. Much love to you all, Judy, Sarah, and Lizzy Getman

Judy Getman <Getdesign@aol.com>
Baltimore, MD USA - Thursday, April 29, 1999 at 21:56:10 (EDT)

April 30
· · · ·

Large day. The great blue dome of heaven has never been at once so vast and so close. Not a shroud of vapor in the perfectly rounded midday sky. Jamien is wrapped in her purple nightshirt with a scarlet ribbon wound round her wrist. Even the birds fall silent at the spectacle of all this beauty. Large night. The moon yellow-orange and pulsing in the last lucent bit of eastern sky. Close enough, you think, to reach out and touch her. Even the peepers fall silent in the wondrous sepulcher of light as one-by-one they, too, round their passage into completeness.

JAMIEN,

On this Maine Spring day I was unpacking the kids' summer clothes and came upon the sweet little dress you gave us for Lila when she came home two years ago. The note you wrote was still with the dress, explaining it was a "grow into." Lila has finally grown enough to wear your little dress. When she tried it on, her eyes twinkled and she danced around the room in true Jamien fashion! It was like your spirit was IN the dress and spread to this three year old when she put it on!

We all wish you comfort and peace on this final journey.

Love, Barb, Geof, Harry, & Lila

Barb Ohland <gohland@ctel.net>
Camden, ME USA - Friday, April 30, 1999 at 00:46:59 (EDT)

The amazing and the terrible balance as you wait for Jamien's passage to the spirit world. Our prayers will be strong as we all contemplate the moon tonight in its fullness.

Jay Aronson <Asaza@aol.com>
Canaan, NY USA - Friday, April 30, 1999 at 12:31:22 (EDT)

Dear Jamien:

My heart beats loudly in my chest and I notice now that I've been holding my breath. I remember fondly a meeting at the Islands flea market. A typical beautiful summer Saturday morning, when slow is the pace. My daughter Kate and I decided to stroll up the hill to discover what treasures might await at today's gathering of crafters, bakers, gardeners, et al. But you know Kate, she has to "dress" for a public appearance. So out came the shiny, leopard-print yard and a half of material, and after SEVERAL attempts she was satisfied with the way it looked. On with the shiny shoes and we were off.

As we passed the church, it became apparent that most of the vendors had packed up and left for the day. That didn't bother Kate for a moment; there were still a few people milling about, and for Kate an audience of one is as good as a million. Jamien was the one. You lavished the sought-after attention as a mother does. Kate-light was reflected back to her one hundredfold. You even asked her to twirl, so you could see all sides. And you know how all-important a twirl can be.

We found our treasure that day and we carried it home in our hearts. Thank you.

Love, Barbara

Barbara Hamilton <barbara@foxislands.net>
Vinalhaven, MME USA - Friday, April 30, 1999 at 12:33:42 (EDT)

Ruby Slippers showed up hanging on our backdoor one mysterious spring day. Emma Rose was quite tickled to try them on. Who left these magic slippers? She knew the Wizzard of Oz *story. Was it the same fairy god-mother, Jamien, that had also left the fairy droppings in our back yard? Alas, the slippers were too big. And so Emma waited two years for them to fit her feet and then proudly walked to kindergarten class.*
David Conover

Dearly Loved Ones,

So many friends when I see them speak of Jamie, and of Philip, and of Tim, Sam, Micah, and James, of tea and trees, of humor and love and parting, of the sea, of death and love, of love and parting, of life and living and living even in parting, and I realize how enormously all you six have touched all of us. I feel part of a great circle which surrounds you and loves you. And as we do so, we are changed, enriched, enlarged, embraced by our embracing, transformed really. I thought of you in your understanding and appreciation of these things, of nature and of beauty, and I find I think of you so often, inspired by such things. Jamie, reach a hand out when you are rising and let my beloved brother know you are there.

Susan St. John <susan&midcoast.com>
Owl's Head, ME USA - Friday, April 30, 1999 at 12:58:43 (EDT)

Dear Jamien, Philip, and family,

The news is out. Everywhere we go people ask, "Have you seen the Web site?" They ask this with a catch in their voices and a hand on their chests. We are all moved by the grace and beauty of this process. We remember the gifts Jamie has brought to our family and our community--her banners, her hats, her words and treats to Lily as her "special friend," the fact that we now exchange every present not in paper but in cloth bags, her kindness to the Polish family who stayed with us, her hard work for good causes. We have not read *Miss Rumphius* for many years but last night it was read in our home again. You have done it, Jamien; you have done "the third and most difficult thing. You have made the world a more beautiful place." Our candle burns and our prayers embrace you.

With love, Anne, Les, Lily, and Andrew

Anne, Les, Lily, and Andrew Hyde <cogger@maine.edu>
St. George, ME USA - Friday, April 30, 1999 at 13:48:44 (EDT)

Dear Jamien and family,

I send all my love. I have not felt comfortable with using the Internet for such personal messages but now can see the true gift that technology may bring you. I have only the deepest sense of admiration for how you, Jamien, have led your family through your journey. I feel that your work will lead them very safely into their own futures.

My mother died suddenly when I was ten; I have three brothers and two sisters. It was and remains a tremendous loss. I still grieve her passing so much. We have all managed our adult lives well. My father was totally crazed by his loss and in many ways we lost both our parents. I so clearly see how healthy your family is and how valuable your time during your illness has been to be with your kids and Philip in such remarkable ways. I really love you and all you have given me and our community.

Thank you and peace be with you, Eliza

Eliza Haselton <Geohas12@aol.com>
rockport, me USA - Friday, April 30, 1999 at 20:25:48 (EDT)

I once got postcards and letters from Jamie as she rowed to Florida with the Outward Bound boat so many years ago. She told, in her lyrical way, of the voyage and the personal trials she dealt with along the way. The card and letters were typical Jamie: reflective, a little wistful at her troubles, and excited by the journey and the people she was meeting. Now, twenty years later, she's off again, rowing to Florida: excited, wistful, and dealing with her troubles with grace.

I'm sorry you're going. I'll miss you, again. Good voyage with fair winds, Jamie.

Rob Miller
Cundy's Harbor, me USA - Friday, April 30, 1999 at 20:55:51 (EDT)

AH, JAMIEN,

I'm with you always! These nightly visits to the computer, kindly juxtaposed with candlelight flickers, are a special treat, but I especially like it when we "meet" outdoors. Like tonight, when atop a quiet Vermont hill we watched the sun set (outrageous pink behind black spruce silhouettes!) and the moon rise--even more beautiful, and more surreal. As is this whole time for me, when your total aliveness is being so lovingly remembered while at the same time your life in this world retreats.

I will continue to write letters to you in my heart and call you on the phone, and I'm sure you'll get them, and we'll both smile. Thanks, James.

With prayers for the final leg of a wondrous journey, and so much love--
Lindy

Lindy Sargent <libnpc@pop.k12.vt.us>
Orleans, VT USA - Friday, April 30, 1999 at 22:34:46 (EDT)

May 1
. . . .

The moon tides are upon us, drawing down the surface of the infinite sea; but there in the moonlight, wave by wave, breath by breath, a hidden seascape appears. This ancient dance turns on the turning moon that peels away the layers of the heart of the sea, and brings gifts on the returning flood.

This morning on Megunticook Mountain, a little past dawn, we startled a moose on our morning run over the ridge in the alpine spruce. Then off on our diurnal rounds to SATs, bake sales, Little League, and juggling at Miss Plum's.

But now the moon is rising again, pulling us outward, outward beyond the edges of our fingertips, beyond our faintly beating hearts, beyond the sentient shadows of night and day, beyond perfect knowledge into something like perfect unknowingness.

DEAREST PHILIP AND JAMIEN AND ALL YOUR BELOVED FAMILY,

Your gifts spill over and over and over and all our lives seem so much richer, so much fuller, so much more connected. Do saints and martyrs choose their fates or is it just "fate"? I dare not ask of the price that is paid.

Thank you Jamie from the bottom of my (Thank God!) breaking heart. I love you all dearly beyond my words.

Susan

Susan St. John <susan@midcoast.com>
Owl's Head, ME USA - Saturday, May 01, 1999 at 13:37:18 (EDT)

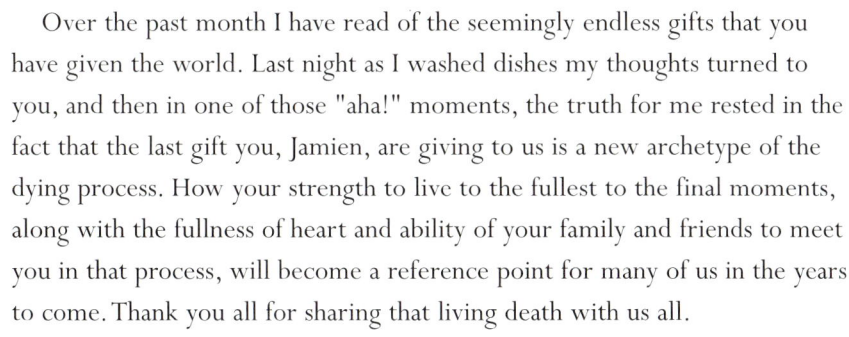

Ariadne, the Sow of my Dreams, 1982

Over the past month I have read of the seemingly endless gifts that you have given the world. Last night as I washed dishes my thoughts turned to you, and then in one of those "aha!" moments, the truth for me rested in the fact that the last gift you, Jamien, are giving to us is a new archetype of the dying process. How your strength to live to the fullest to the final moments, along with the fullness of heart and ability of your family and friends to meet you in that process, will become a reference point for many of us in the years to come. Thank you all for sharing that living death with us all.

My question remains…how can we bring this honor to more of the human beings passing through this earthly existence? Your blessings shine through the sun and the moon.

In true awe, Bridget Qualey

Bridget Qualey <Stetson@Mint.net>
Camden, Maine USA - Sunday, May 02, 1999 at 08:23:19 (EDT)

DEAREST JAMIEN,

I laugh when I remember the baby shower you joined in on many years ago when I was pregnant with my first child. We had not availed ourselves of the conveniences of modern medicine and did not know what we were expecting (gender wise!), but you gave me a sweet pair of rose-colored knitted pants and told me they were certainly exchangeable, but you had "a feeling" I wouldn't need to exchange. You were right, and you greeted Caroline's arrival with some home-baked breadsticks and a joyful banner you made, which has adorned her room wherever we've lived.

One day she will ask where it comes from, and I will tell her about you.

Love, Cathy Willauer, David, Caroline, John, and Archer

Cathy Willauer <dowzerw@aol.com>
Cumberland, ME USA - Sunday, May 02, 1999 at 15:28:41 (EDT)

DEAR PHILIP, JAMES, MICAH, TIM, SAM, JAMIEN--

Just managed to get to a computer after a week on the road. AMAZED how things are unfolding. This has long since passed ordinary miraculous. It is awesomely miraculous. Keep your hearts open. You are never out of my prayers. I'll be home on Tuesday. Happy birthday to Micah and James.

Love, Cynthia

Cynthia Bourgeault <treaven@saltspring .com>
Aalt Spring Island, BC Canada - Sunday, May 02, 1999 at 16:50:40 (EDT)

DEAR JAMIE,

My thoughts are with you every day. Last night I was remembering the huge, beautiful banner that you made for our Good Wooden Boats from Maine business. We took it with us to many boat shows and received more compliments on the banner than the boats. Plus who can forget your Pies for Peace program. Such creative, energetic ideas and projects.

Much love and peace, Jan

Jan Taft <taft@mint.net>
Camden, ME USA - Sunday, May 02, 1999 at 18:24:12 (EDT)

May 3

• • • •

Jamien died peacefully in her sleep at 2:00 a.m. this morning. It seemed the last decades of her life were compressed into the last days of her journey and then into her last hours, like watching single grains of sand blowing away with the last whispers of wind, like a flame with nothing left to burn suspended in air for a long moment when the dance of life and death is over.

Yesterday, as she tugged and tugged at her mortal coil, the expression on her face changed more than once, and her whole faced lifted as she raised her eyebrows. Maybe in surprise.

She loved us all well, and we loved her powerfully. We will remember her in a thousand thousand moments, and at a memorial service May 15 in Rockport. Details will follow.

All love,

Philip, Tim, Sam, Micah, and James

Aloha

Bruce
Belfast, USA - Monday, May 03, 1999 at 05:50:52 (EDT)

The First Universalist Church in Rockland will open its doors tonight at 7:00 p.m. for an informal gathering of community to think of Jamien…a time to light a candle, say a prayer, speak if the spirit so moves…to be there for Jamie and her family. All are welcome.

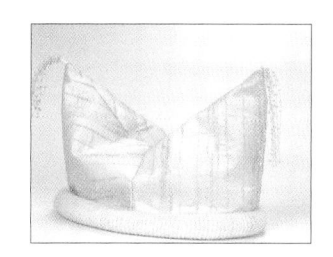

mimi bosntein-doble <mimibd@mint.net>
camden, me USA - Monday, May 03, 1999 at 09:41:39 (EDT)

Henny Penny, 1986

PHILIP, LEE, DICK, TIM, SAM, JAMIE, MICAH, BRUCE,

Our hearts go out to you. We join you in bidding Jamien a bittersweet farewell. Thank you so very much for sharing with us Jamien's long passage, and for letting us share with you our love for her and for you. Her strong, strong heart and her enormous Life Force, so much larger than Life, was a beacon that burned with a fierce, powerful radiance. It burned on when her body could barely hold it, it burned with a passion for you, her family, whom she loves with an enduring, unquenchable flame. That Love and that Spirit hasn't died; only the chalice is gone. She fought so very hard to endure the ravages of her disease so she could stay with you as long as humanly possible.

Now her Spirit endures within you, within all whom she touched, even within all she continues to touch as the ripples of her influence continue to spread, multiply, and reverberate to distant shores and people who never even knew her. It's a force astonishing to witness and experience.

Please count our family as among those eager to be there for you in any way we can.

The Scott Family: Anita, Geoff, Tana, and Kyle

The Scott Family <scotts@mint.net>
Camden, ME USA - Monday, May 03, 1999 at 12:21:58 (EDT)

TO JAMIE'S FAMILY:

The "it" has finally happened. I can almost hear all of us who were surrounding and supporting you (and there were more than you know) emitting a long, sad exhale of breath. Your creating this Web site was such a gift to us who live beyond the realm of your home. Do you know how much it meant for me/us to be able to be with you in this way, and to form a new community with others who were focused so poignantly upon you?

It has changed me (and I see others), your generous sharing of such a private pain, in that it allowed us to experience the most "real" thing that we all must face sometime. Thank you. My loving thoughts and sympathy go out to all of you now, and for future years without the sparkling light that was Jamie.

   love, Allison Cooke Brown

Allison Cooke Brown <@ bpb@ceimaine.org>
Yarmouth, ME USA - Monday, May 03, 1999 at 14:36:58 (EDT)

   The earth mourns and the heavens and angels sing--
   Thoughts and prayers are going your way on angels' wings

Lynelle Vaughn <lvaughn@superiorcoffee.com>
Newton, MA USA - Monday, May 03, 1999 at 14:54:44 (EDT)

   In my first spare moment today I wanted to share with Jamien how I enjoyed connecting with her once again through Sam this weekend. We were together at Miss Plum's, me with two lambs from Kelmscott, he with juggling, flashing knives. But the news on your Web site of the conclusion of your challenge in this space means my message is too late? I can't believe it.

   Jamien's spirit, I believe, is stronger than this change. I must tell you, J, Sam was great on Saturday! He drew the biggest crowds, passers-by looked on and marveled. He is yours, Jamien, evidence of celebration, as are all your children and family.

   I'll always cherish a few moments on a bench with your Dad. His peace and calm when talking about you was profound, flowing with pride and love. We are all so lucky because we knew you. I'll forever sing of your spirit in my heart.

   Adieu, my friend.

Kim Fletcher <development@kelmscott.org>
Lincolnville, ME USA - Monday, May 03, 1999 at 15:03:22 (EDT)

Whew! What a thrill that life was and what a ride her passing!

Phil Crossman <tidewater@foxislands.net>
Vinalhaven, Me USA - Monday, May 03, 1999 at 17:58:07 (EDT)

Dear Philip and sons,

We prayed for you in Mass today. May God be with you all in the depths of your sadness. May you feel His presence, His divine mercy in your hearts, and in the hearts of those who love you.

Jamien is a rare gift to the many people she knows and loves. It has been said that grief shared is divided and that joy shared is multiplied. May you know these truths with all your hearts. May God bless you all.

Love, Bill Burke

William Burke <WLB3RD@aol.com>
Needham, MA USA - Monday, May 03, 1999 at 18:32:28 (EDT)

Such a tribute to the possibility of living through the soul. I will remember this time with a sweetness, a sadness, and a longing to find the grace to live each moment of my life like a bird singing in the night.

Nancy Hanrahan <oakleaf@midcoast.com>
Rockport, Me USA - Monday, May 03, 1999 at 19:50:36 (EDT)

Fruit Flag 1979

Dear Jamien,

Although i have only met you a few times, your spirit and light have been an inspiration to me in ways i cannot begin to tell you. Thank you for that. Pass well and know that your essence--your spirit, light, and energy--have been multiplied by four in your lifetime and have been absorbed by all those

150

who have encountered your presence, no matter how briefly. You are a gift. Thank you, Jamien.

    peace and love, monica shields

monica shields <mhesters@yahoo.com>
maun, botswana - Tuesday, May 04, 1999 at 03:35:44 (EDT)

May 4
• • • •

Monday was, as one of Jamien's great friends said at Church that night, "a good day to die." After a sunrise service with Jamien's five men and boys circling her perfect body, we gave ourselves up to the universe's ascending lightness of being. We piled ourselves into two vans with Gramma and Grampa, Uncle Bruce, and Aunt Wendy and circled round the harbor to sit on the far side with a Market Basket lunch on our knees and a making tide at our ankles. If we could just hold onto this moment forever...suspended between being and nothingness... maybe it would all be well. But we know better; the universe has already moved a whole heaven and earth since Monday morning and the tide is ever turning in rhythmic patterns and the silent music of the spheres we cannot hear or see but in the inner chamber of the heart and in the stillness of the dead.

To Jamie's family,

    From the moment I met Jamie at Middlebury so many years ago, I was struck by her free spirit. Whenever Jamie was around, there was fun, laughter, and a new adventure. She was unencumbered by inhibitions that restrained so many of us--so able to soar in her creativity and love. She is truly a free spirit now and as the tears flow down my cheeks, I think perhaps she was one of the rare angels that come to earth.

151

I cannot tell you how through the years her perfectly timed phone calls inspired me--as if she knew when I needed her. As we struggled together with twins, illness, raising boys, I thought we were cosmically linked. Now I understand that all of us who knew her felt the same way and were uniquely uplifted by her spirit. She had divine gifts. Our prayers are with you.

Love, Jeannie, Fred, and all the Burditts

Jeannie Burditt <samjakebo@msn.com>
Canton, Ct USA - Tuesday, May 04, 1999 at 10:43:34 (EDT)

Jamien's leaving us evidently occurred at the change of the early morning tides, just a half hour or so after Full Sea and into the ebb. The Full Pink Moon (named for the spring flowers) had gone from "full" into its wane only a couple of days previous. Then I found this Web site and read of Jamien's "visits" with family and friends who have died before her.

Jamien with Sam and Tim, returning from a fishing trip on **Fish Hawk** *the Island Institue boat, 1988*

I bet her boat was a beauty, an elegant wooden sailboat like my father's old Herreshoff 12-1/2, *Shadow,* in which I once joined him for a full moon sail that might have looked something like Jamien's the other night--pure magic of moonlight on water, a "transporting" equal to no other, almost soundless on the water, and slow enough to take one's time in appreciating every beautiful, nightlit sight along the coast of Maine.

When someone we love is dying, the beauty around us comes into such spectacular focus. Once they've died, the trick becomes to sustain that same love and appreciation in our daily lives--as Jamien so often reminded us to do.

love, Martha (& Taylor A. & the kids)

Martha White <ncrown@midcoast.com>
Rockport, ME USA - Tuesday, May 04, 1999 at 11:59:26 (EDT)

DEAR PHILIP AND FAMILY,

   We have been interlopers in this passage that you have shared with such grace and dignity. Your entries each day reveal a man with courage enough to be open, to be filleted, to be revealed. This has all been such gift. We remain thankful in prayer. If nothing else, this life is sure vivid.

Chris Burr <cburr@burr-assoc.com>
south natick, mass. USA - Tuesday, May 04, 1999 at 12:15:42 (EDT)

TO EACH HEREIN,

   Yesterday May 3, attending Mass, I smiled to see in the Roman Catholic calendar that it was the feast of saints Philip and James. With only slight rewording, happily included in light of Jamien, here is the Prayer after Communion:

> "Father, by the holy gifts we have received,
>
> free our minds and hearts from separation and barriers.
>
> With the apostles Philip and James
>
> may we see you in sons and daughters
>
> and be found worthily living life in time and in eternity.
>
> We ask this through the transformation of Christ, each
>
> one sent to light the way."

Bill Halpin <mygbrook@midcoast.com>
Camden, ME USA - Tuesday, May 04, 1999 at 13:08:41 (EDT)

   Last year, eleven days ago, my father died in my arms. In the wonder, confusion, grief, and mystery of that moment, grace happened.

   May you know deeply, now and in the months and years following your beloved's transition into another, peace that surpasses all understanding.

   My prayers and love are with you, AM

Ann Marie Almeida <annmarie@camden.lib.me.us>
Rockport, ME USA - Tuesday, May 04, 1999 at 17:59:14 (EDT)

The last time I saw Jamien was in the supermarket. She was choosing oranges. She stood bathed in the glow of that bank of sunshine, smiling, gently assessing the fruit with her knowing hands. It was lovely to watch.

Elizabeth O'Haverty <ohavhope@midcoast.com>
Hope, Me USA - Tuesday, May 04, 1999 at 19:27:17 (EDT)

Didn't know your Jamien until meeting Peter the day she died. Wished I had met her. I'll be planting a ginkgo out in the forest in her memory.

My thoughts are with you, Rick

Rick Churchill <rickc@megalink.net>
Newry, ME USA - Tuesday, May 04, 1999 at 20:37:01 (EDT)

Dear Philip and the boys,

I feel blessed that I knew Jamie during her too-brief time here. Even my son remembers her visit to California, because she had sons who could sleep outside in the snow! She will be truly and deeply missed, but we are all so lucky to have known such an amazing friend, mother, wife, and woman.

My thoughts and prayers are with you all.

Love, Hatti Saunders

Oakland, CA USA - Tuesday, May 04, 1999 at 22:01:40 (EDT)

Dearest Jamien,

This is the first night I bid you good night searching the sky for some sign of you. I know you're there, with your beautiful smile, just beyond my reach but not beyond my heart. I miss you, many miss you, and I try to think of ways to be strong; strong for those who are left behind. I'm trying, but it's really harder than I thought it would be. So I will keep my eyes looking heavenward so the tears won't fall.

    Goodnight, dear Jamien.

Melissa Winstanley<winstanly@aol.com>
Wellesley, MA USA - Tuesday, May 04, 1999 at 22:55:13 (EDT)
[Melissa Winstanley is Philip's sister.]

In Memoriam

. . . .

While we clicked on every day and ached, laughed, cried, and delighted in the crazy quilt of Jamien's earthly and spiritual connections, our computers were growing a soul. How can such an impersonal medium be the vehicle for such a deeply moving experience? It must have been Jamien.

Deborah Shinn, May 7, 1999

Emma's Castle, 1978

May 5-8
• • • •

Tuesday was hard. Where to go? To work, to school, back to bed? We gathered the day in little pieces. Knowing that waiting till Wednesday to go back to wherever we go would be no easier, we trundled off as if life goes on. On Wednesday while Sam's science class took a test, he wrote a beautiful elegy for his mother, which he will read at her service next week. And when Thursday came, we conspired to deliver a plate full of brownies to a chemistry class for Tim, who turned seventeen to speed him through the afternoon's moments of blood sugar deficit. And also to honor him who had traveled across his mother's heaven to get and be next to her in the final weeks of their lives together. I have never been more proud of the wings of youth unfolding and growing stronger with each day.

DEAR PHILIP,

  today i looked at the pictures in the gallery and realized that i smiled for the first time in days. thank you.

    love, sara

sara gilfenbaum <sarag@sad50.k12.me.us>
thomaston, me USA - Wednesday, May 05, 1999 at 13:51:54 (EDT)

  I don't know whether you, Jamien, or your family knows me. I'm new at our church, but I feel I know you well through all you and your family have shared, but more through the incredible depth of feeling that surrounds you. As I read people's thoughts here, it's clear that your spirit is still growing.

  On Monday, I stood on the beach at Birch Point. The air and the water moved gently and it was suddenly very clear to me that you were present--in the light, in the sounds, in the feel of the air, in the molecules all around me--

and I breathed deeply. Thank you for touching my life and letting me see your soaring spirit.

Jeanne Klainer <jklainer@aol.com>
Rockland, ME USA - Wednesday, May 05, 1999 at 16:12:22 (EDT)

  A dear friend of mine (the mother of a friend of Jamien's) urged me to come to the site. Bless you. What a gifted, gifted woman she clearly was, who was able to pass along--and thus multiply--her deep heart gifts. I will take her inspired tea invitation and bring it along into this part of the world. May Jamien's life force be carried on into this world.

Irene Borger <musegrl@aol.com>
Los Angeles, CA USA - Wednesday, May 05, 1999 at 20:39:22 (EDT)

    to a fellow writer who shared many an op-ed page…
      your words always had that seemingly paradoxical spirit
      of idealism and pragmatism…
      head in the stars, feet on the earth…
      such a lovely balance…
      i thank you for them….

doug hufnagel <fiftytwo@mint.net>
Belfast, USA - Thursday, May 06, 1999 at 09:26:20 (EDT)

  What grace and hard work, joy, fun, and pitiless determination show in Jamien's life. It's a sorrow to have her gone, but her example is still here.
  Prayers and blessing to Philip, Tim, Sam, Micah, and Jamie.

David and Sydney Hall <mudhen@midcoast.com>
Hope, me USA - Thursday, May 06, 1999 at 14:38:27 (EDT)

159

It is clear from what I do know about Jamie's life now, that she was truly married to Amazement, and I feel that if there is one thing I can do to honor her, it would be to live my life in amazement with her. Our job has become great and will take the strength of all of us to carry on sharing her inspiration and enthusiasm. Polaris to the north is steady in the sky while the stars appear to revolve in a great celestial circle.

Keep your eyes on the stars!

To her family and her friends, I offer my prayers.

Namaste, Sally Thibault

Sally Thibault <bythesea888@earthlink.net>
Owl's Head, ME USA - Friday, May 07, 1999 at 08:36:03 (EDT)

I think back to the banner that Jamie made for me when I first started attending the University of Richmond. It reminds me of a great Vinalhaven tradition of waving banners from the lawn as a greeting, or as the case may

Micah and Jamie greeting the Vinalhaven ferry, 1994

be, a farewell to those riding the ferry to and from the island. Many times it was myself who was coming in on the ferry, and Jamie was among those waving the banner on the lawn at Vinalhaven.

Well, as surely (and sadly) as I am waving farewell with that banner that Jamie made for me years ago, no doubt Marcy, Uncle Norman, and countless others are waving hello on the other side.

My deepest condolences.

Sincerely, Jim Harris

Jim Harris <jimharris@erols.com>
Morristown, NJ USA - Friday, May 07, 1999 at 12:24:21 (EDT)

DEAR PHILIP, LEE, DICK, TIM, SAM, JAMIE, MICAH,

Thank you and bless you for sharing Jamien's passing with her friends through this Web site. While we clicked on every day and ached, laughed, cried, and delighted in the crazy quilt of Jamien's earthly and spiritual connections, our computers were growing a soul. How can such an impersonal medium be the vehicle for such a deeply moving experience? It must have been Jamien. Love and peace to you, Deborah Shinn

Deborah Shinn <shinnde@ch.si.edu>
New York, NY USA - Friday, May 07, 1999 at 12:41:29 (EDT)

DEAR JAMIEN,

I knew you such a short time, about two months. You hired me to clean your house once a week. I was so honored to do it, and to be in your presence in your last weeks of life. You shone with a beauty and radiance that left me awestruck. You went about the task of dying with such a natural grace that will always be a great inspiration for me. You touched me deeply and I thank you from the bottom of my heart. You are an angel.

    love and light to you and to everyone you've touched, Wendy

Wendy Meacham <wmeacham@acadia.net>
Northport, Maine USA - Friday, May 07, 1999 at 17:16:18 (EDT)

GREETINGS.

    The last few weeks have been truly inspirational. Jamie's strength, love, and courage remind me of flowers which have gone to seed. A gentle wind blows and the seeds are scattered to take root and grow again. The cycle never ends. So, too, will Jamie live on through her good works and the inspiration she has been to us all throughout her journey. May we all strive to live each day as an adventure, nurture those around us, and help the world we live in to shine!

Donna Miller Damon <Donna_Damon@onf.com>
Chebeague Island, ME USA - Monday, May 10, 1999 at 13:11:25 (EDT)

DEAR PHILIP,

    Nightly I have visited the Web site, to check on Jamien and from time to time to send a message of love and support. Your updates seem to reach right into my heart. Actually, they reach into the heart of the universe, opening it wide, and daring anyone not to feel it. My heart goes out to you and your sons. Your plans for the service seems perfect. I hope that the service brings your family healing and strength. Although I will not be physically present, I intend to join you in prayer at that time and then to say goodbye to Jamien by sharing a cup of tea.

    All my love and support, R. Buxbaum

Robert Buxbaum <Rbuxfree@aol.com>
NY, NY USA - Tuesday, May 11, 1999 at 00:08:42 (EDT)

Dear Philip,

Caught up with the Web page this morning, which only confirmed what I already somehow knew, winging my way home yesterday over about three-quarters of the United States, amidst towering, sun-sparkled cumulus, and a green, fresh earth…even a dusting of new snow on the mountains. What a vast, majestic day for a spirit to soar free….

You have all done your jobs very, very well. As this amazing flood tide of grace, exhilaration, communion, and Mystery slowly recedes to the more usual ways of perceiving and doing, may you all be protected as you gradually unwind, and may you ease gently into this new season of your lives. On May 15, I will be in solitude in Rafe's old hermit cabin in Colorado. (Rafe was my hermit teacher, whose death three-and-a-half years ago initiated me into the gentle art of journeying with a beloved beyond the grave.) Miraculously, the monks are letting me use it to keep the ten-day fast between Ascension Day and Pentecost (May 13-23 this year). This always seemed to me one of the most awesomely mystical times in the Christian year, when the physical body of Christ has finally departed and the new manifestation, the indwelling spirit, not quite arrived.

The boundaries between heaven and earth are so permeable in this little space, and in the intense listening, one catches a glimpse, if very still and very lucky, of that most amazing of snow leopards, the resurrection body of one's beloved. I will hold Jamien and all of you deeply in the stillness of that day.

We're all deeper than we thought we were, aren't we? A bunch of crazy, hard-driving, self-preoccupied hippie punks and transplants have become poets, mystics, and saints in spite of ourselves. Did Maine do that to us, or was it God?

Be well. Breathe deeply.

Love, Cynthia

<treaven@saltspring.com>
Salt Spring Island , BC Canada - Tuesday, May 11, 1999 at 10:32:48 (EDT)

I've been remiss in not checking sooner for the news I was sure would be there. But it's not too late to join you tomorrow in spirit as you gather at the memorial service--which seems so perfectly planned. Like many others, I'll have a cup of tea tomorrow morning and think of what I've learned about Jamie from this Web site. And I'll offer my prayers that Philip and the boys will be given the strength and wisdom to carry on, following the path that Jamie blazed. What a legacy she has left us all.

    Franci

Franci Vinal Farnsworth <farnswor@middlebury.edu>
Brandon, VT USA - Friday, May 14, 1999 at 09:07:52 (EDT)

"Hello," you said. "You do not know me. My name is Jamien. I live next door and knew your mother. I think you need some help. I have a truck. I am not working today." That was at seven o'clock in the morning last September after I had been up most of the night clearing out my mother's house, which had been sold. I was coming out of the garage. There you were.

"I will be back in an hour," you said. "I just always take a walk early in the morning. Can I bring you anything when I get back?"

Tea, fruit, and English muffins arrived in abundance. You made the decisions about what not to keep of my mother that I could not make myself. You gave me the strength I needed to part from my past. Little did I know you were ill, too.

You told me about your favorite piece of land on Beech Hill in sadness and shock that you had seen a For Sale sign. My husband and I saw the property the next day. We are now the owners.

You suggested we hold a vigil for my mother to welcome in the new owners and release her spirit. Sunday evening two days later, Peter, you, Nancy Foster, and I lit a candle for her. You had prepared a few beautiful words.

We all spoke and shed a tear. The next day we learned Mum, who had been ill for many years, had died during that moment of remembrance.

Finally, Jamien, how extraordinary to have known you only those three days. What joy and peace you brought into our lives. And one thing more. I began reading your memoriam today wishing I could be with you tomorrow. You were born the same day and year as Peter, my husband. We are all connected. May the peace be with you that you gave to so many others. May we follow in the goodness of your walks. May our land on Beech Hill forever be your sanctuary. I know Peter and I will see you there very soon.

Much love to you, Jamien, Victoria Oscarsson Heimann

Vienna, Austria

Victoria Oscarsson <oscarsson@netway.at>
Vienna, Austria - Friday, May 14, 1999 at 13:00:58 (EDT)

Jamien with Micah at the twins' christening, Hurricane Island, 1988

DEAR PHILIP AND FAMILY,

We did not have the privilege of knowing Jamien but she touched our lives in such a sweet way by thinking of our daughter. We were extremely fortunate to have a child several years ago. Jamien took time out of her busy life to share in our excitement and wonderment of it all and sewed a beautifully whimsical hat for our daughter, named Jamie. To this day, that hat is a favorite and adorns any number of dolls and animal friends. Jamien had quietly, without fanfare, recognized and celebrated our greatest accomplishment in this world.

Philip, thank you for sharing Jamien's magnificent tributes with us via this extraordinary Web site and may you and your sons take some comfort in knowing that Jamien touched so many lives in her own uniquely wondrous way.

Diane Harrington and Bill Marshall

Diane Harrington and Bill Marshall <harrington_diane@hotmail.com>
Stuart, FL USA - Friday, May 14, 1999 at 15:38:48 (EDT)

165

Mer, Mere, Merci

> There
> is no
> explanation for death;
> for life
> Here
> it is, yes
> on the water, flowers
> lovingly our looking
>
> (after Jamien, 15 May 99/wfh)

wfh <mtgbrook@midcoast.com>
Camden, ME usa - Saturday, May 15, 1999 at 10:02:57 (EDT)

Memorial Service

JAMIEN ELISE MOREHOUSE
FEBRUARY 4, 1951 - MAY 3, 1999

Rockport Opera House

MAY 15, 1999

Selections From The Speakers

Flowers cast into Rockport Harbor from the Memorial Service

What I Learned from my Dodge Caravan

A letter from Jamien
March, 1999

Dear Friends,

    I am taking advantage of this rare opportunity to write you a final letter. For starters, I will remind you that I love you all and that I consider myself very lucky to be in this circle of friends. And if you wore a hat today, I thank you. You look terrific.

    Here is my brief story. It might be called, "What I Learned From My Dodge Caravan."

    For ten years I have been looking for a miracle. What form it was going to take, I couldn't tell you. A lightning bolt? A message spelled out in the clouds? Perhaps I'd awaken from a sweet dream and be in perfect health.

    During my search I was also bullied by life. I changed a lot of diapers, shoveled snow, ate rhubarb pie, paid bills, signed report cards, gave haircuts, found my place in the bleachers at ballgames, drank tea. Pretty much the same as everybody. I loved the day-to-dayness of my life--mostly--and felt very blessed to be the mother of four wonderful boys and the wife to Philip. We did lots of laughing together, as well as a bit of crying. All our lives are made up of so many little stories, most of them a bit dull, but which add up to the pictures of our lives, actually perfect little collages. My story was, all things considered, a blessed one. Balanced. Happy. Loved. Sustained.

    It was in the still mornings of my days that I continued my search for that elusive miracle. I became superstitious. I collected lucky stones and always had my eyes open for four-leaf clovers. At night I'd lie by the woodstove and try to glean a message from the shifting embers. I lay on my back in the yard

Jamien's boots, a gift from friends after her mastectomy and chemotherapy, 1989

and waited for shooting stars. I regularly left the lawns of sleep and joined the night world, always waiting for a sign.

The sign actually came to me in my Dodge Caravan when I read, for the thousandth time, the message in the rearview mirror: "Objects In Mirror Are Closer Than They Appear." The sweetness--and humor--of these words was their familiarity. Didn't I know I was living a miracle? That in the ordinariness of my existence I was already connected to the stars, stars above and stars below? That haircuts and diapers and rhubarb pie are miracles-- even bills are miracles--just as all of you are miracles? They, the miracles, are closer than they appear; sometimes they are right in our laps, little diamonds everywhere.

What I share with you here is not so profound--many know about this miracle stuff. It just happened to come to me as I drove my van backwards. It was like hearing a bird sing in the middle of the night.

It's no accident that we all lie nestled together in the curves of the universe. We are all part of the mind of God. The world turns as we sit here together today; it turns as we sleep. We are tugged by the forces of celestial tides. Time folds in on itself and outward again in gladness as we spin around, each of us an utter miracle in a sea of tiny white stars. All is well.

Love,
Jamien

This letter was read at the Memorial Service by Jamien's cousin, Wendy Harris.

James Conkling's cover for the Memorial Service

The Rabbi's Gift

    Once upon a time there was a large, beautiful abbey. The abbey had a famous choir, a library stocked with important works of literature and theology. The nuns who lived there were known throughout the land for their kindness, their spiritual wisdom, and their many talents.

    By the time of our story, however, the convent had fallen upon hard times. People had lost interest in spiritual wisdom. Other more lucrative careers beckoned to the women of the age, and fewer and fewer young women came to the convent wishing to offer their talents to the glory of God. Eventually the library fell into disuse. The choir stopped singing, for lack of listeners, and the nuns gave up thinking and writing about God, and fell to bickering among themselves. The abbey had become a sad, poor, and shabby place.

    The Mother Superior, the oldest of the nuns, was hobbling through the forest one summer day when she happened to come upon a small hut in a clearing. Smoke was coming from its tin chimney, and a smell of fresh baked muffins was in the air. "Oh, I know who lives here," the Mother Superior told herself. "I remember someone telling me all about it. There is a rabbi from the synagogue in town who comes out here to the forest from time to time to meditate and refresh himself. Come to think of it, I have heard that the rabbi is very wise. Perhaps he can tell me what can be done to help our abbey survive the coming winter?"

    The rabbi welcomed the old nun into his hut. He poured her some tea and offered her a muffin. They chatted for a long while, and it was very, very pleasant, but at last the rabbi had to admit he had no advice to give the Mother Superior.

    "The only thing I can tell you," he said, "is this: The Messiah is one of you."

    The Mother Superior pondered this in her heart, all the way home to the abbey. Over that night's meager dinner of cold cabbage soup, she told the other nuns about the conversation. "What can it mean?" the sisters asked one another, that night and for many nights afterward. "How can the Messiah be one of us?"

    Which one of us? Do you suppose he meant the Mother Superior? Yes, of course, it must be: She remembers all the old times, and the old ways, has read all the books, and written a few as well. It must be her.

But wait. Wouldn't the Messiah be young? The youngest among us is Sister Elizabeth. But Sister Elizabeth is always so gloomy, fretting and worrying about the least little thing. Of course, sometimes the least little thing turns out to be important, and it's always turned out worse for us when we failed to listen to her. The Messiah could be Sister Elizabeth. Unless it's Sister Margaret.

Oh, she is so silly, always tripping over her own toes. Messiahs aren't clumsy. Well, but Sister Margaret truly has a sweet spirit. And she has always been able to draw and paint so beautifully, such a creative person would be chosen by God. But what about Sister Susan?

Oh now really. It couldn't possibly be Sister Susan. She never speaks, except to apologize for something she didn't do. What sort of Messiah is that? Ahh--but you know, though she is quiet in her speech, when she sings, the sound of her voice makes you think such glorious and noble thoughts. It could be Sister Susan…or Sister Margaret…or Sister Elizabeth…unless…(and this was the oddest thought of all)…what if the Messiah is ME?

As they went along in their ordinary days, the nuns were pondering the problem ceaselessly. And just to be on the safe side, they began to treat one another with extraordinary respect. At the same time, they began to treat themselves with extraordinary respect. They began to take everyone's thoughts very seriously, for instance, and wrote them carefully into books, for any of these might be the thoughts of a Messiah. In fact, they began to do all their ordinary work deliberately, carefully, because--you never know!--this might be the work, the poetry, the gardening, the song, or the dream--of the Messiah.

Many people from the town took picnics to the forests near the abbey on Sunday afternoons. Soon these picnickers, without even being quite conscious of it, began to notice a change. There was beautiful singing floating over the abbey walls, flowers bloomed in the windows, and beautiful, hand-sewn flags flew from the rooftop. There *was a new and wonderful atmosphere of extraordinary respect around the place, and the people liked it very much. They brought their friends, and word of this wonderful abbey, radiating love and respect, spread throughout the countryside. A talented young musician came to visit the abbey, and asked if she could stay and serve the order with her music, and soon more young women arrived, eager to lend their energy to such a place. Within a few years, thanks to the rabbi's gift, the abbey was a busy, thriving center of light and love for the whole land.*

Adapted by Kate Braestrup from an old Hasidic tale and read by her. "I have changed the story in a minor way for this service," said Kate. "Those of you who know the story will understand why." Kate, a neighbor and friend with four children, lost her husband, a State Trooper, in a car accident. She is currently enrolled in the Bangor Theological Seminary.

Elegy for My Mom

For weeks before Monday, the day after my Mom died, our small house on Maple Street had been full of people. Hospice workers, grandparents, friends, helpers, and the most meaningful presence, Mom. Yesterday, as I arrived at home after a laborious day in school, I came to a completely empty house. There was no one. I thought about the situation, and realized that this was the first time that it had ever been like that. There was always a presence to come home to. Always. Whether or not my mother was actually home at the time I came didn't really matter. She would always be there soon enough. I remember, before all these complications came about, coming home always to a friendly call from her work room. "Hello, Sam!" Always, it was so happy, and full of vibrancy. I miss her so much. Even in the last weeks, the last days of her life, when she could hardly speak, she was still there. Her presence alone was enough for me. To be able to walk through the curtain and just look upon her beautiful, content, happy, and radiant face was enough.

The day we got home after a family memorial picnic, and she was gone, it was a shock. I would never see her mortal body again. Last night, as I scrolled through

people's posted massages on jamien.com, I came across one that struck me, I realized that it was true. It said that Mom must have been one of the very few angels who came to the earth, to our lives, for a stay. Her creativity, love, care, and humor bloomed like a beautiful flower, and spread and unfolded into the lives of so, so many. On every person she met, on every person she spoke with, every person she corresponded with, her amazingly wonderful energy rubbed off like pastel colors, and inspired. Observing her artwork, her magnificent wooden fish, her colorful, flowing banners, begin to show what kind of a person she was. The things she was passionate about, she would put so much into, and always the results were spectacular. One of the things she was so passionate about was being kind and open and loving to all people. I cannot express how lucky I feel to have lived so closely with her for the time I was allowed. Anyone who came into any kind of contact with Mom was a better person for doing so. She loved and was loved by more people than I can even understand. She was an angel. I love my mother.

Sam Conkling
May 5, 1999

Think Globally, Act Locally

Hi, I'm Bruce Morehouse, Jamie's little brother. First, before I start, let me say that in an effort to be able to speak I have assiduously avoided emotional content. I've left that up to the other speakers.

I'd like to take you down a brief reflection on Jamie's life. Being a database, computer type person, I went at it in a strictly mathematical method. I'm going to give you a statistical analysis of Jamie's life based upon the last forty days of postings to the Web site http://www.jamien.com. I'll tell you how I managed this feat. First, I downloaded all of the messages and loaded them into a database. I sorted, analyzed, dissected, and otherwise distracted myself from some very deep thoughts while doing this.

That were about 600 messages posted. These messages came from six different continents (North America, South America, Europe, Asia, Africa, and Australia) and most of the United States. I figured that there were probably more people visiting the site than those 600 people (especially since a few of those posted more than once), but I wasn't sure. I then called up the Internet service provider and he sent me the statistics on the site jamien.com. But before I give those numbers to you I need to tell you about two Internet terms. "Hits" and "lurkers."

When you visit a Web site, the host computer records the number of times your computer asks for information. This is a "hit." On jamien.com, it was estimated that, on average, there were ten hits, or requests for information, every time someone visited the site. There are those people who visit or hang around a Web site, but never make their presence known by posting a message. These are the "Lurkers."

Here, then, are the numbers. Are you sitting down? For forty days, from March 25 through May 10, 1999, jamien.com received over 175,000 hits or an estimated 17,000 visits. Now I only visited a couple hundred times, so I knew there were a bunch of lurkers out there. Perhaps others visited more than I did (it was a many times a day ritual, after all). Here I've got to explain yet another Internet term: "domain." The text to the right of the "AT" sign (@) in your e-mail address is called the domain. Everyone has a unique e-mail address, but lots of people share a domain name ("@aol.com" is one of the bigger ones). Guess what? There were about 4,500 different domain names that visited the site. So there were a lot of lurkers out there after all! I was right.

Now, these numbers are pretty impressive of themselves, but the content is absolutely staggering. For starters, there are some truly eloquent writers (though I wasn't able to quantify this, I'm quite sure it's true). The writing was so eloquent that it prompted over thirty people to write in who didn't even know Jamie! My favorite one of these messages, typed in all uppercase letters and probably from a teenager, read:

"MY NAME IS JAMIEN TOO. THIS SITE REALLY ROCKS!"

I then took all the messages, squashed them together, and made a list of every word used in the whole pile. I grouped the words by word root and counted how many times each word root was used. I then sorted this list. Now this analysis won't stand up to rigorous scrutiny, but it does give you a good idea of the concepts people wrote about.

There were about 7,500 different words used. After dropping off the thirty-one most frequently used words ("of," "and," "the," "in," "a," etc.), the most used word root had to do with "thinking," "thought," "thoughts," and so on. In fact, words with the root of "think" occurred more than twice as frequently as any other word! This is significant. Jamie got a lot of people thinking.

Other significant words I'll list and you can draw your own conclusions: friend, 8th), thank (23rd), tea (24th), heart (31st), touch (35th), through (54th), into (57th)--very important words denoting motion--wonderful (56th), great (58th), spirit (59th), beautiful (60th), peace (61st), people (66th), world (73rd), light (74th), inspiration (92nd), gift (110th), new (111th), and together (126th).

The last term I'd like to introduce is the "Harmonic Convergence." The Harmonic Convergence took place back in August of 1986. It is a Mayan Indian concept. The idea is that the harmonic convergence marked the beginning of the messianic age for the world. But, instead of there being only one Messiah, there are a lot of enlightened people. These people in turn enlighten others who enlighten others and so on and so on. It's sort of like connecting the glowing dots. This is not a top-down idea but a bottom-up idea. It appeals to me quite a bit. Jamien was one of those glowing dots, illuminating the thousands of people she touched.

Jamie was one who truly believed in and acted upon the dictum, "Think globally, act locally." She has been illuminating many lives during her life, bringing smiles and a better way of being to so many folks through this wonderful method of "contagious good thoughts."

Never doubt for a moment that a thoughtful, committed person can change the world for the better. Jamie has.

Bruce Morehouse

"I'd like to think that some of her has rubbed off on me"

Jamien's coded button art letter, 1990

Mom was very big on raising "her boys" to be responsible human beings. She was determined to bring us up in the best way possible, and her clearly defined rules of responsibility and accountability were the cause of many disciplinary measures, which, at times, seemed very frustrating to my brothers and me. I can clearly remember one particular incident that was certainly not at all funny to me when it happened, but looking back, I can recognize its humor.

About four years ago I got my first modem and I wanted to be "connected." I got an account with America Online, which was a very expensive service to use back then. Not only did I have to pay per-minute long distance fees, but also the cost of using AOL's services was $3 per hour. The first two months of service were great. I was completely oblivious to the fact that I was running up an enormous bill, and I was somehow under the impression that my parents would be paying for my account anyway. When the bill finally arrived in the mail after those initial 60 days, Mom approached me with it. It ultimately totaled over $400. I seem to recall a particular $80 phone call to a place I had never heard of: the Seychelle Islands off the Coast of Africa. And I was informed, much to my dismay, that I was completely responsible for paying every penny of it back. So I went to work for my mother--for an entire year.

I am not what you would call a very thrifty person. Money seems to disappear mysteriously whenever I come into contact with it. Mom quickly devised a strict payback plan. I was to pay her $15 per week or else she would start adding interest. I was not allowed to spend money on myself, and I also wasn't allowed to use my modem, which I had just bought with $70 of my own money. Mom kept a weekly chart detailing how much I still I owed, as well as how much I had paid back. Needless to say, it was a hellish ordeal.

It seems that I was always learning things from Mom, like how to be responsible about money. But she had a lot of other things to teach us as well. From an early age *she taught us independence and how to take care of ourselves, even how to take care of our mistakes. I feel immensely proud to have been a part in her life, and I'd like to think that some of her personality has rubbed off on me. I also feel a closeness to the multitudes of individuals whose lives were changed in some way when they spent time with my Mom.* **Jamien.com,** *her Web site, is a testament to the incredible effect she had on those she made contact with, and I am glad to have played a part in maintaining the site.*

Tim Conkling

"Moon Hill Downeast"

Jamien grew up in a planned community known as Six Moon Hill in Lexington, Massachusetts. We were brought together by shared interests and objectives in child rearing, neighborhood care, and involvement in Town affairs. It was the children who bound the neighborhood together most effectively. In 1954, when there were eighty-five children under the age of eleven years, an article in Vogue magazine concluded, "On Six Moon Hill where doors aren't locked and everyone calls everyone by his given name and the first person met in any one house is apt to be someone else's child...families have something in common. They want a special framework in which to raise their children."

We would block off the cul-de-sac road for coasting parties and street square dances. Annual Easter egg hunts proved to be a competition between the children and the neighborhood dogs...And the dogs often came off as the winners, with their sticky marshmallow snouts to show us that they were there first. Kite flying was an annual picnic event down on the abandoned golf course. Winter ice skating picnics on the frozen swamp pond at the base of the hill seemed extra special even though the menu was Dinty Moore stew and corned beef hash. Sundays were for pick-up soccer games...All ages encouraged to play and team sizes unimportant. And during summer

Dick, Lee, Marcy, and Jamien at Company Point, Vinalhaven ca. 1955

evenings, children were seen, dressed in their nighties or pj's, carrying their pillows, wafting through the warm half light deciding and then reconsidering just exactly whose house they were really going to end up in for the night. It was a lovely way to grow up.

It was this essence of family and neighbors which Jamien sought for her own family. At one time in Jamien's adult life she said to me, "Mom, you never prepared me for the real world." I was startled and defensive. She said, "I thought that everywhere I lived I would find the same values as those of Moon Hill." Ultimately she moved to Rockport...She found all of you...Living in many neighborhoods and not just on one street. She grew to love many, many new friends who shared the beliefs and values which she pursued with such passion. I believe that each one of you...friends who gave so unstintingly of love and support...represent that which she held so dear, valued so highly, and practiced every day of her life. You represent her Moon Hill Downeast.

At one time recently she said, "You know, Mom, I like to write letters. Because I am left-handed I like to think the words flow right from my heart to the paper." The many loving words from you to her surely flowed from your hearts. Jamien is smiling.

Lee Morehouse, Jamien's mother

Family portrait, Rockport, 1990

Maiden Voyage

I.

During the darkest hours of night,
Always when I am deepest under,
A small animal begins gnawing
Inside the plaster walls by your bed.
And always you are wide eyed, as if in surprise.
You walk through the house, gathering the cares of the day
Like little piles of laundry you leave at the doors of our morning.

II.

I like to think of our first winter at the Egg House
When I was away in the woods of the Baskahegan.
You battled the barn rats through a long siege
Until one finally crept into the cupboard, knocking a jar to the floor.
You went naked in terror to the kitchen in high heels
And surprised it between the tomatoes
Where Tanya broke its neck in her jaws
And laid it deftly at your feet.

III.

But now the gnawing goes deeper.
You walk through the neighborhood,
And finally into the hills
In your white nightgown and housecoat.
Sometimes in the hills at night
You take off your coat and gown
In the dark of the moon.
Which makes me smile.
Diana the Huntress,
Coming to death's hearth like a lover,
Giving yourself up like a virgin to the night.

Philip Conkling
May 13, 1999

Remembering to Breathe

. . . .

I long for this Web site to to live on.

To have the tempo of caring continue its song.

Yet each day...the voices grow fewer and fewer..

From one who reaped the joy

of your giving, I thank you.

Bridget Qualey, May 21, 1999

Jamien's watermelon flags, Lane's Island

I was drawn to check the page again this morning and can't read all the messages--only a few at a time--because of the intensity of the love that is expressed there…the love, the pain, the beauty..I didn't get inside the Opera House yesterday, but even hearing the service while sitting outside on the park lawn, overlooking the harbor through the leafing trees, well, it was an extraordinary experience. And what a special, special family. I feel so lucky to have been touched by all of them, to be a part of the enormous community Jamie drew to her. With all of this, I keep on seeing Jamien's smiling eyes and lips as she spread her radiance whenever, wherever, I saw her.

Willie Eaton <willeats@midcoast.com>
Camden, ME USA - Sunday, May 16, 1999 at 07:14:09 (EDT)

Dear Philip and the boys,

Saturday was just right and I admire you all, each one, for being able to share yourselves with all of us in celebrating Jamien's life. I loved many things about the gathering on the shore, not least of which were the funny responses to Philip's moving poems to Jamien: "My husband couldn't write a poem about me if his life depended on it!" "Does voice mail count?" "How about e-mail?" Obviously, we each share our hearts in the ways we're able, but how wonderful to consider the many forms, together.

One quick thought, to pass along. When my father die, (Dec. 97, also of cancer), I worried that I would forget something of his voice or face or presence. I haven't, and I've stopped worrying about that. Also, a wonderful comfort for me were the dreams of him that began about six months after he died. They are infrequent, but often very joyful, and seem like small "visits." I'm told that's common, and that the six months' time is often the case.

Take care.

Martha White <ncrown@midcoast.com>
Rockport, ME USA - Tuesday, May 18, 1999 at 09:38:28 (EDT)

DEAR PHILIP,

So many people, so much to lift us up, so hard for boys to sit on stage for sooo long, so many tones to connect souls to the living and to the dead, but once you began to read your poems to one so loved I longed for you never to stop. And then to read of the openness of heart that you brought…it rang a truth reached only when one is free enough to scatter one's self to the wind of human compassion. I long for this Web site to live on. To have the tempo of caring continue its song. Yet each day I visit to collect the harvest of cyber symphony and the voices grow fewer and fewer. Our maestro is gallivanting with the Gods. It's so hard to call forth that pulse out of our own day-to-day dimensions. I will continue to seek out your poetic perceptions of your transformed existence.

From one who reaped the joy of your giving, I thank you.

Bridget Qualey <Stetson@mint.net>
Camden, Maine USA - Friday, May 21, 1999 at 21:37:42 (EDT)

In the corner of the downstairs room where Jamien lay so peacefully, we've gathered little lucky pieces, golden icons and statues of fat Ho-Tai that sit between two candles of the Virgin de Guadelupe that burn for three days and more. The picture of James, her lovely hands cradling a cup of tea, sits next to the box of her ashes, some of which have been spilled under a yew the Mustang Ranch Runners, my runner's group, planted on the morning of her service, and others cattered over a new garden in the backyard. In the box of ashes we found the arrow-shaped Buddha she wore round her neck, and are deeply comforted by its return voyage back into our living hearts. Somehow the lights flickering underneath the silk-screened prayer flags are comforts, too, when we return. Like this Web site, where we return from time to time to remind ourselves of the deep springs of love from which we drink when we share the cup of sorrow.

May 22
. . . .

183

May 23

Remembering to Breathe

Friends ask me about life after death,
But what do I know?
I can't say what dark weight
Hangs on the left side
Of this caged heart
Disturbing a rhythm
The body has spent its lifetime
Not remembering.

Yesterday just before noon,
A wind from some other continent
Blew through the eaves.
Beginning as a murmur,
It punched through the diaphragm,
Like a sigh from a thousand nights ago
That gathered to gale force,
Then settled back
To a dull moan
Before exhausting itself in sleep.

Everything is all right
The mystics say.
But no, you know it's not like that,
Not like before.
Because neverness does not stop
Where it does not arrive.
It just rounds the line of the horizon

And keeps reappearing
Like a hole in the heart
Out of the blue nowhere.
Just keep breathing in,
And breathing out.
You don't ever want to forget that.
You can't ever forget that.

              PWC

Thank you, Philip, for your poetry in prose and verse. I think about all of you often and have sent several friends to this site for the tea ceremony, to share an incredible life gone too soon, to see a community in action. And I've discovered several Maine friends from other parts of my life than Middlebury who know you. The world is truly small these days. I hope that your in-person community is still very much there for all of you in ways those of us in distant parts cannot be.

   Peace to all, Sallie Sprague

Sallie Sprague <ssprague@cc.wwu.edu>
Bellingham, WA USA - Monday, May 24, 1999 at 23:50:53 (EDT)

May 25

Lost and Found

Can you believe it's been three weeks,
Sam asked, eyes to the ground,
The light fluttering through
His 15-year-old misted eyelashes?
No, I said, I can't.
It seems almost last century,
Since his mother's flag-waving spirit
Was shred in the winds.
But in the next breath, Sam told this story:
He and his brother had just been
To Rockland on an errand,
When turning a corner saw
A toughened skater on a board
He thought was his.

So they quickly parked and rounded up
To confront the bag-kneed boy,
Identifying the stars Sam had cut
As his signature in grip tape,
And special wheels and trucks
Ordered from the coolest catalog ever.
I don't want any trouble,
The boy mumbled in giving up
The stolen prize
He swore he'd been given
By someone else a year or so ago.

The sweetness of this small triumph
Is nothing next to what is
Lost, and lost forever.
But a stolen memory reclaimed
Quiets down the storm
That still rages on inside
Beating against the lie
That nothing is irretrievably gone.

       PWC

Tim Messsler, Tim and Sam Rockaway, Lane's Island

Osprey, Penobscot Bay, 1978

Thanks, Philip, for your beautiful, moving poem. It has me remembering that somebody (Voltaire, I think) said, "It is no more suprising to be born twice than it is to be born once." Where and in what form, he didn't speculate. In Jamie's case, perhaps everywhere and in every form. It is hard to imagine that such a spirit could ever be constrained to a single box. It is easy to imagine that she is in everything now. In fact, at the moment, I see her flying over the cove with the osprey.

Bob MacLaughlin <wordplay@midcoast.com>
Cushing, ME USA - Tuesday, May 25, 1999 at 09:23:23 (EDT)

I've been away but found myself drawn back to this site as soon as I could after returning home. I'm saddened that the messages are dwindling, but felt blessed to read the updates of the memorial service and your ongoing lives. I know that eventually the communion here will end--but oh, how I long for a "hard copy" to refer back to as I need it--and I will need it.

Carol Petillo <carol.petillo@bc.edu>
Vinalhaven, ME USA - Tuesday, May 25, 1999 at 12:58:46 (EDT)

DEAR DEAR PHILIP AND BRUCE AND JAMIE C (AND JAMIE M TOO!) AND MICAH AND SAM AND TIM AND LEE AND DICK AND ALL THE REST OF YOU,

I hadn't expected to come back here, after so beautiful Jamie's service last week, yet I ask all of us what I ask myself. How do we transform the focus that has been on Jamie to the more immediate field? How does/can grief transform the expression of our love? The focus of our love? We who have given tiny pieces to this Web site must learn how to give it elsewhere. I ask myself: how can we learn to make a difference wherever we are? I do not know the answer to that question, but it is one I find worthwhile, because all of you Conklings and Morehouses are facing it in such an unimaginably large way, that the least the rest of us can do is to address it in our own smaller ways. I think many of us also want to make a difference. Sometimes it can be with casseroles and flowers and notes, but it also must be in the form of reaching out a loving hand, a loving heart, wherever we are. Every day. And sometimes I think, "Can this make any difference?" with a sob in my throat. And then I think, "Well, it surely can't hurt."

    Love and Love, always, Susan

p.s. We held your pew for you last week, and were buoyed up by so doing.

Susan St. John <susan@midcoast.com>
Owl's Head, ME USA - Tuesday, May 25, 1999 at 23:19:58 (EDT)

    Having gone through great loss myself this past year, my heart is with your family. It is a strange but great privilege to be shaped into finer form by the enormous pain that you must carry now. Nothing goes to waste and the mysterious is ever present. This much I have discovered so far.

Sherry Dec <sdec@midcoast.com>
Waldoboro, Me USA - Wednesday, May 26, 1999 at 19:37:40 (EDT)

May 25
• • • •

Dear Family, Friends, Visitors, and Everyone,
So much to hold in the heart; so much to connect, so many trails that touch this Web site and leave the purest vibration of life that takes the sting out of death. Then, too, the boys and I have been trying to reinvent our lives between mornings and evenings, trying to be careful with each other and not to disturb the universe any more than it has already been. I am further humbled by the jobs of motherhood; by the sheer complexity of knowing at all times where four other souls are at this moment and where they're headed and what they've eaten or not and

which has a music lesson or art class and who will drive them from point A to point B. Half the world knows all this already; it's just the rest of us who learn more slowly that are catching on. We've been greatly helped by a pair of young women from town, Sandy and Susie, who come in afternoons and help get dinner and homework started and are kind and cheerful.

Tim went off to the Prom last weekend, with a date no less, looking suave in his dark blue jacket and slacks set off with a blood red tie. Just the day before, Sandy, our household angel, showed him how to slow-dance. "I mean where do you put your arms?" he needed to know and she helped him figure this mysterious bit of adolescent passage. Jamien would have loved it.

The thoughts of the head haven't migrated yet to the heart. I still see an interesting piece of "junk" and think to pick it up for James, knowing that she could create something beautiful with it. How differently I see the world because of her. What beauty she created through us on that great day of her memorial in Rockport. What power a single person has to affect the world.

Bruce Morehouse baggedmail@acadia.net
Thursday, May 27, 1999 at 13:14:20 (EDT)

I haven't visited the site for several days but was once more moved to tears by what I read. The site has clearly served many purposes. Besides a touchstone for remembering the joy and sharing the burden of the grief, it also seems to have been a giant teach-in consciousness-raising about family, friendship, death, and life. As much as Jamie was the catalyst, I suspect she might have also found something to grow from in this communal experience that perhaps was ultimately just another extension of Moon Hill.

What the site has taught me more than anything else is to always focus on the glass as half full while never forgetting it is also half empty. I continue to think how to apply what I learned here to a wider world and think it would be part of Jamie's legacy if I ever accomplish that. Whatever you decide to do with the site, it is a little miracle that I'm sure will stay nestled in all our hearts who were your honored guests, part of this remarkable journey.

Aviva Rahmani <ghostnet@foxislands.net>
Vinalhaven, Me USA - Sunday, May 30, 1999 at 12:19:36 (EDT)

PHILIP,

Time has slipped by so quickly and we have still not crafted the words in our minds and to our satisfaction, to express our sadness at the loss of your life partner and dearest friend and helpmate. I've watched my mother over eight months since my father's death and know that she is on a journey that no one can travel for her, or even with her. Yet what sustains her are the still occasional hugs, words of sympathy, and especially remembrances of Dad that she receives from people. She has read and re-read the cards and letters and draws comfort from others' expressions of their admiration and affection for

Returning from New York City Marathon, 1998

Dad, a sharing of sentiment not fully expressed or even realized in his life.

    We didn't know Jamie and had met only Sam, and so we didn't want to intrude on your family during her final days. But Peter told us about this site and we visited it and read your exquisite expressions of emotion and accounts of how a family manages to live day to day, remembers to breathe in and breathe out, as you said, in the midst of such pain. Whatever you do with the site, you have an irreplaceable treasure here in your personal record of these days, and I'm sure in your friends' and families' responses. I want to thank you for your courage in sharing with us in this way. You have given us all a wonderful gift, possible because of the ironic coincidence of technology and your own and I'm sure Jamie's creative souls. This site has been a comfortable way for many, I'm sure, to check in with you without being obtrusive, and allowing you the control over intrusion and noise that you all needed and I'm sure continue to need.

    We have just celebrated the fifth anniversary of our son Russell David's death, birth, and burial. As I read your eloquent expressions of grief, I feel that old wound in my heart tearing open and the tears are flowing. You have reached deep within me and made me feel again, made me re-connect with a vulnerability that reminds me again of our fragility, our place in the universe, our very essence of humanness. It hurts to go there, but it is vital that we do so. Nothing reaffirms life quite so much as deep, incredible pain. Thank you again. With much love and concern,

Janice and David <waweig@nbnet.nb.ca>
Waweig, RR 6 St. Stephen, NB Canada - Saturday, June 05, 1999 at 08:58:45 (EDT)

June 6

* * * *

Lady Slipper

Late afternoons seem to draw the feet up the hill over Rockport Harbor, up behind the cemetery where once you found a wild rock garden and

began bringing friends for tea. How you found this place I'll never know, but there must be a story to it of how your feet were drawn, too, up this hill over Rockport Harbor when you were out walking either early or late, as was your habit when the circling pain threatened to close in. And there you found amid the tangle of overgrown paths, a hint of wild abandon; amid mute broken stones, something that begins to suggest stone-lined edges of paths, then stone steps that lead deeper into the secret wood...

On the steep backside of this south-facing slope, part way down and half hidden in green shrub (not just any shrubs but exquisitely sited yews and rhododendrons) the path twists into a little hollow ending at a large stone table--a stone altar with stone seats around its edges. And hidden in this deep woods are the most delicate perennials and a stupendously orange-pink flowering azalea. How can this be, I wonder, dumbstruck? So I sit and wait for some sign, some whisper, some way of knowing what this is for, why you brought me here.

And while I waited, a cotton-eyed seedpod carried by a will-of-the-wind floated dreamily by. And I listened to the bird calls and wondered which had found your voice and taken it up in its singing. And slowly my chafing spirit quieted down, but was not lifted by these sights and sounds. And so I turned to go, and crested the hill when I was momentarily blinded by the late long rays of the afternoon sun and paused for a half instant to get my footing; and there at my feet, in the glow of memory's orb, was the full rosy blush of a lady slipper, a singular thing of beauty edging the trail that someone long ago had carved out of a distant misery.

Ah! I see, there you are! And how magnificent an afternoon it has been waiting to see you and finding this fleeting, fleeting moment, the color of beauty, the color of your rosy cheek, at this exact spot where you have walked. Yes, now I am beginning to see!

So many times the beauty of this spring has offended me when I think of the pain of losing Jamie. But I too found a moment when she was with us but I was reluctant to share it with you until I read your last update. My son Sam has just been diagnosed with diabetes, and instead of fleeing to Maine for Jamie's Memorial Service I was home learning to deal with yet another physical intrusion into my loved one's well being.

That night, while I was feeling spiritually exhausted and selfishly devastated in missing a moving farewell to Jamie, a huge black bear came right up to our glass doors and put his face to our windows. We all gathered to watch as she ambled casually in our backyard, stopping to sniff the flowering almond bush and looking back at us in the light. She was so beautiful and casual and happy -she lingered far longer than most wild creatures. And so my friend researched bears looking for a sign from this visit. She found that bears, according to Indian legend, can harbor and protect human spirits. So for me that night, Jamie came to visit and bring me comfort once again.

Perhaps I am grasping for more than is out there, but it makes sense to me, knowing Jamie, that she would visit both as a lady slipper and a bear. Her spirit is safe and powerful.

Love, Jeannie

Jeannie Burditt <samjakebo@msn.com>
canton, ct USA - Monday, June 07, 1999 at 17:21:55 (EDT)

I don't usually let my emotions control. I usually watch and wait, and things work out. I try to be helpful, thoughtful, cheerful; maintain a good Zen position. I keep thinking about Jamie and her family, and I know things will work out. I visit this site for a sense of shared grief/love. But it usually leaves me feeling wrung-out and ill-equipped to communicate feelings.

I guess I wanted to let you guys know that I'm thinking about you and have been as moved by this experience as I have by anything else in my life. Philip has given me a renewed interest in poetry and trying to express true feelings in a meaningful way.

I hope the site continues. It is an inspiration, and makes me think better of people and of myself.

hollis tedford <watrshed@midcoast.com>
Waldoboro, ME USA - Thursday, June 10, 1999 at 17:43:52 (EDT)

DEAR PHILIP,

Last year, at about this time, I spent a few days in our woods attempting to paint the lady slippers. This year, when I went back to the spot where they have always been, they were gone. I absorbed my disappointment and was continuing my walk when I began to see them in new places. And now I've been seeing new ones almost every day--suddenly they seem to be everywhere, just not where they were before. You've provided the explanation. This site continues to weave the most amazing tapestry.

Much love, Jeri

Jeri Hamlen <mhamlen@mediaone.net>
Wayland, MA USA - Thursday, June 10, 1999 at 23:19:15 (EDT)

Tim, Jamien, and Sam, Eagle Island 1985

June 13

A Bird Singing in the Night

I was not dreaming, although I had been asleep. I was wide-awake and listening, and it came again...a bird calling in the night. How do you describe a sound you cannot repeat, from some living thing you do not see, from somewhere out there in the darkness? It was not the kind of song one might expect from a careening night hawk or hunting owl; no, not like those calls I know well. Just two notes, changing pitch and deeply musical. It sang once more, very clearly, and very close. Then silence slowly wrapped its arms around me for the voyage back to death's dream kingdom.

But I knew what this singing was about. A few weeks before she died, Jamien had called me to her bedside and wanted to tell me something. She had been sleeping most of the time and was only awake for short stretches between the drops of morphine that fell on her tongue like rain. Then, though, she was wide-awake and lucid. And said this: "I want you to tell Wendy to add a sentence to the letter she will read at my service. Right after the part where I wrote, 'Objects in Mirror Are Closer Than They Appear,' tell her to add: 'It's like hearing a bird sing in the night.'"

Nowhere are these two notes, hanging large and full, repeated just twice, four sounds of the ineffable that stir the heart deeply and tug at the cords of memory. Do memory and desire play such tricks on the mind? Yes, of course. But that is the lesser truth; the larger truth is I know that life flows on in endless song, above earth's lamentations. I hear the real but far-off hymn that hails a new creation.

Dear Philip,

I continue to visit this site regularly, yet not as compulsively as before. In many ways it seems to have become more personal, and yet it also seems to be more universal.

Streaming through the cosmos, this conversation between the living and the dead, the living and the living…There exists an odd sort of bashfulness for me…you put forth the beauty of words experiencing, exploring, sharing in this road back into "normal" life, sort of in a generous fish bowl. We site visitors know you, and yet at some level we remain blank and unknown faces to you. Words passing into and through cyberspace, when in my case I live a mere few miles away. To share and yet at some level still pass in the night, since I don't believe that I have ever met you personally.

Bless you for your continued sharing. I pray that your pain and your awakening to the song of bird in the night will birth self-knowledge that will inform your new and what must be lonely path.

Warmly,

Bridget Qualey <Stetson@mint.net>
Camden , USA - Sunday, June 13, 1999 at 20:54:41 (EDT)

It's beautiful to see the tendrils of new beginnings creep quietly in. I feel like a smile is just starting to turn up its edges. It feels like dawn, and the beginning of a new day.

A friend
Vinalhaven, USA - Monday, June 14, 1999 at 16:23:54 (EDT)

Detail of Meg's Field 1978

For the first time this summer, my children are gone for the entire day. I was up at dawn with lists of all the things I was going to accomplish today, two of which were to write to Jamie's parents and send a check to the Vinalhaven Land Trust in memory of an Awesome Woman. I found the Web address and thought I'd check it out. Two hours later, after tears and some chuckles, my list out the window, here I sit, nearly transformed by a woman I knew for a long time but all too briefly, and by all the lives she touched. Every time I encountered Jamie all those summers on Vinalhaven--at the Library, at sailing, wherever--after we parted, I always had the feeling of wanting her to stay a little longer just to share what the world needs more of --love, laughter, and positive energy.

I will be giving my children extra big hugs when they come home today. Thank you, Jamie.

Ann Peterson Ramee <bramee@aol.com>
Savannah, GA USA - Thursday, June 17, 1999 at 14:44:13 (EDT)

June 19
• • • •

In the Empty Plate Is a Gift
The simple story you told of the empty plate shadows me through these days, although you only told it to me once before you died. When you told the story, it had no moral, at least that you spoke through the flooding tears of remembrance, but I think I finally got it.

You were at your Grandmoneri' house, your Victorian grandmother's, your mother's mother's house, which I imagine as full of beautiful dark walnut and oak furniture, lace curtains, and antimacassars on the arms of the overstuffed chairs and sofa. It was Thanksgiving and you were maybe eight, there with your sister, cousins, aunts, uncles, parents, in the living heart of your extended family.

You were passing around the candied fruit; it was after dinner. This was the most special moment of the holiday for you, this special candy, of beautiful, delicate, jellied red, green, orange and lemon-yellow semicircles lightly sugared with a sharp sour rind, the most delicious thing in all creation. You were being the good child, the perfect grandchild, passing around the full plate of multi-colored candy to everyone. And when you had completed the rounds, the plate was suddenly empty, there was no piece left for you. Worse yet, no one had even noticed that you sat back down and stared at a huge and awful emptiness.

When you told me this story, we were having a hard time. You were sick and we were afraid you wouldn't get better. The boys were aching and knew everything. I used to wonder where your goodness came from; it was so large, so unaffected, so light-hearted. I think of your life in this story; in your knowing from the beginning that there is no reward for selflessness; it's not a deal you make with God for which you are rewarded. There is only goodness or not; the thing itself, by itself. You either pass the plate or you don't, and when it comes back round to you and is empty, in that miraculous empty plate is the biggest gift you will get in life, that you will give in dying.

June 27

RAVEN'S GORE

The steep stone beach is hot,
And a yellow wind stirs eddies against
The skin and bones of Brimstone Island.
We have steamed all morning
To be here among the gulls
That scream at us from above.

I choose to bring the children here
To celebrate this Father's Day,
Knowing we will not find you here;
Knowing we can only find you here,
Where we've come to sit so many times before
At this entrance to the island of the dead.

Visits to these cliffs years past always
Felt so large, and time so immense;

Expanding out over the whole ocean
Like inner vision from an immortal hawk.
Days when little boys climbed the hills,
Heads poking out from brown grasses
To gain some purchase on this place
Where one world meets the next.

Two decades or more ago
Here before I even knew of you,
Edging around an outcrop,
High above the breaking surf
I came face to face with a raven
Hunched on a narrow ledge
Staring balefully out to sea.
Suspended and motionless,
Neither of us dared breathe
Until the spell was broken
And the raven flung itself
Out into the void,
A broken wing trailing uselessly
As it fluttered to the sea,
And paddled outward bound
With its one wing waving.

Instantly the gulls are alerted, seeing
Something living, but only partly living.
They wheel and scream:
Raven down! Raven down!
And swoop on the sodden creature

To square accounts for once
With this ancient bird of death.
On its back, it rises up
To greet each new tormenter, again and again,
In the agony of its impending doom,
Meeting each feint with an eerie cry
Until a clever pair time their assault
From fore and aft,
And break its neck from behind.

As we stand here with your ashes,
Three ravens grok about on a lone spruce
And then two more wing in from the west.
Five ravens now over the five of us.
Oh how your numbers have grown!
Here now with you gone
But forty-nine days ago.

I wish there were some way to make peace
Amid these warring fates
That contend for this most sacred place.
Is it your restless spirit or mine
That unleashes these winged furies
Where the sea just pounds the shore?
But, oh!, the sheen this endless rote gives
To brimstones rolled and tumbled
And piled soul-deep on this beach,
Polished parts of lifeless creation,
Like pieces of vajra,

That adamantine substance said to cut
Through both wisdom and desire.
Though now in each chamber of stone
I still hear that defiant call
I will carry in the inner ear
With my love to the grave.

PWC

Dear Conklings,

    Here it is midsummer, and I took an extra moment today to check in on the Web site. I think of Jamien often, especially when I am doing some of the most seemingly mundane chores of tending to household or children. And I say to myself how very precious these moments really are, how we really don't realize it until we no longer have them.

Annie Kiermaier <lbak@mint.net>
W. Rockport, ME USA - Sunday, July 18, 1999 at 17:03:35 (EDT)

Sam and Tim outside Jamien's room, Rockaway, Lane's Island, 1984

Your Room

July 25

I crossed the wooden threshold
Of your enormous summer room,
Looking over golden heaths
Onto miles of empty ocean.
There's a first for everything,
These days; so many, many firsts
Since you finally flickered on
To some greater reward.

Outdoors now is quiet
Where once the pheasant cocks
Woke the dawn from little hillocks
And called us out of
Our sleepy summer coils.
They too must have succumbed
To the winter or the gun.

The heart heaves heavily
On these stone shores of memory,
Spilling wave after wave
On the rosy lips of our beach.
What could endure here
At this sea-worn edge?
Except gifts from our cells
To ourselves;
Of four strong boys
Who fill an empty ocean
With all the antic energy
From grand and broken dreams.

This could be enough, I think
But for your flag waving spirit
That slats at the eyes
In this stinging summer gale.

PWC

Dear Philip,

    I didn't have the honor of knowing your wife, at least not on this physical plane. However, I will tell you that her spirit--no, it would be correct to say the spirit of her family and friends--has touched a place deep within me that is hard to define. It doesn't seem enough to say thank you for your brave reflections on a very painful period..I lived on Vinalhaven for about nine months. Lane's Island is the place to which I return, if only in my mind, whenever I have the need for quiet retreat. This site is such a lovely tribute to her life. I wish you peace.

Teri Kolton <tkolton@aol.com>
Charleston, sc USA - Sunday, July 25, 1999 at 18:42:32 (EDT)

DIRECTORY ASSISTANCE

August 6

Just under the inky black
Surface of the deep,
The boat's phone shorted
This dream into consciousness.
It swamped the holds,
Seeped through floorboards
To lap at my night-gloomed berth.

From that deep under place
I had dialed four-one-one,
Asking for a connection
To only God knows whom.
When you miraculously answered
And said quite distinctly,
"But Philip, you know who this is."
Your full voice, your steady gaze
Flooded up in waves of grief.
I tried to answer,
But was somehow voiceless,
Pushing only air from pounding lungs
Through a stricken passage
Of the gaping mouth,
Like a cod gulping air on deck.
Yet I know you heard
The hoarse wind shriek
Through my rigging
Like an offshore gale.

      PWC

While I'm not sure what draws me, I find that in quiet moments this site brings peace and calmness. Thank you.

Jean Jackson <jjacks@ttlc.net>
Stratham, NH USA - Saturday, August 07, 1999 at 20:59:07 (EDT)

Today is a back to school day…a day I would usually share with Jamie as our cars waved, our kids bumped in hallways, and fresh off our islands we looked with mixed emotions as the kids moved away from us at the end of another summer. I miss these life moments with my friend and town is emptier without her. I am grateful this site continues.

Deb Meehan <maplesyrup@midcoast.com>
Camden, ME USA - Monday, August 30, 1999 at 15:35:55 (EDT)

HELLO, PHILIP.

Thank you for this Web site. I lost my father June 21 of this year and miss him terribly. He lost his wife 33 years before, and was left to raise three little girls. If you do half the job he did, your children will be the luckiest children in the world.

its not an easy job. But you'll get through it. One day at a time.

Lynne C <Mrs c225@aol.com>
Pittsfield, MA USA - Sunday, September 19, 1999 at 17:16:33 (EDT)

Jamien and Jamie, 1993

October 4
• • • •

Today would have been our nineteenth wedding anniversary. I wrote this poem two years ago on this day for Jamien who was travelling across Siberia with her eigthty-three year-old friend Margery on her last great adventure. Jamien had always believed that she had lived a previous life somewhere in Mongolia, a place she always hoped to visit. The Altai

Mountain Range separates Russia from Mongolia, and during this trip she got within a handful of miles of the Mongolian border.

Siberian Anniversary

I
A late malingering Indian Summer dome
Of rich hues of gold slanting light
Flickers early and late along the harbor fringe
Kindling little fires of faith,
As you race eastward into winter.
II.
Early snows lash your face in Moscow.
While further east, beyond the frayed ends of the Silk Road
Lie three ends of the earth:
Academgorodoc, Novosibirsk, and finally the Altai!
You and Margery, a pair of peregrines,
Ravaged and ravishing,
Beating into the eye of the winter sun.
The great Trungpa said: Outward bound is inner journey.
III.
The morning you left
The light was like a sleepy cotton nightgown
Whitened in the easterly eye of the morn.
Your beautiful battered body
Was back lit in pools of shimmering form:
Making tea, feeding birds, watering flowers.
Three found fragments from a lost vase.
Can you not know how exquisite you are?

IV.

Seventeen years I think with four beautiful boys,

And still my heart is in my throat…

Before this great, good, fleeting fulsomeness

Of scarlet cowgirl boots in umber Autumn light

Loses its rosy blush

And we are molds moldering in the leaves,

Beyond these last beaches of desire,

We build our castle of brimstones

Back on the fiery lips of our cove,

And feel the rote, and live the rote, and love this rote

Beating eastward into the rising of the moon.

Beating eastward into the rising of the moon.

PWC

Dear Philip,

The Heavens are shedding chilling tears on this your wedding anniversary. I know this date brings the aching pain of Jamien's absence sharply home to your heart. But I hope, beyond the inevitable pangs, you can sense all around you the warming rays from the reverberating echo of her powerful Spirit, her deep tenacious love.

May the many legacies of Utterly Unique Jamien and the remarkable partnership you shared bring you a fond smile as you let them instill in you the warmth of knowing she is still here, around you and your family, in the community to which she gave so much, and in her friends who still love her so much and hold dear their daily thoughts of her. The anniversary of your partnership is indeed cause to celebrate. Warmest wishes!

Anita

Anita Brosius-Scott <scotts@mint.net>
Camden, ME USA - Monday, October 04, 1999 at 13:37:12 (EDT)

I truly, deeply hope that, if this Web site ever closes, it will be because the wonder of it all has been lovingly put into book form. This site is my "touchstone" with my spirituality.

Thank You...

Karin <kgt1940@webtv.net>
Yarmouth, Me USA - Sunday, October 10, 1999 at 11:36:17 (EDT)

October 30 NIGHT BLIND
• • • •

    The buck was down on its knees
    At the S curve of Old County Road.
    His head and big rack craned back
    Against his creamed body in the dark.
    A long line of cars had stopped,
    As worried mothers and friends
    Stood around like at a crucifixion,
    Headlights glaring off into the night.

    I thought I know how this feels:
    Is my heart broken, or was I just nailed
    To this road by a hammer in the night?
    And who are all these people staring
    Into dark corners of this pain?

    The strange tableau just hangs there,
    Stripped of its beginning and end.
    Nothing but a night-blinded beast
    Down in the middle of its road
    Amidst the low buzz of consternation.

                              PWC

November 29 *Against the backdrop of November's gray forms, our lives are stripped back to bone-bare trunks and rattling limbs waving in the wind. Into this stark picture comes a fantastic piece of news: the Farnsworth Art*

Museum in Rockland is renovating the old Newberry's Five and Dime on Main Street and will name the new gallery space the Jamien Morehouse Wing!

The boys and I are thrilled to know that Jamien's flag-waving spirit and endlessly restless creative energy will wander immemorially through the new gallery spaces where she once loved to shop for cheap birthday gifts and holiday treats. The first show of the millennium will focus on island art, combining Jamien's great love for the Maine islands, especially Vinalhaven, with some of the most enduring contributions from artists who have worked here and been transformed by the great magic of being "On Island."

The dedication and ceremony unveiling this great new space and exhibit will occur fittingly shortly after Memorial Day weekend, 2000. We hope many of Jamien's friends and family from near and far will be on hand to help celebrate.

December 15

Last Saturday, the mail brought a letter to us from Jamien, which she wrote last April unbeknownst to us, and asked my sister to send. It was a beautiful letter but a shock to receive, and even harder to read. I thought some of you might like to know about it.

Your Christmas Letter

The mail brought your letter today
Addressed to me in a hand
I would have recognized anywhere.
I gaped and gasped, could hardly grasp

That it was written long months ago.
You remind us to retrieve
The boxes full of memories
Christmas candles and the creche
That may make the season light.

"We got a wonderful start together,"
You write in a river of words that flood
From hearts to brimming eyes,
"So continue growing into
The strong family of men you are,
And when you think you've had enough
Remember you can always tap
Into the deep love we started with."

Christ, but I cannot think you now
Suspended like a star somehow
Alone and cold and bright.
But see you here in words afire
That dance across the book of time
Before your pen ran out of ink.

Oh, the nights are long and cold,
And dark comes creeping in.
But even so I also hear
Two pure tones of song from you,
A bird calling in the night.

PWC

wow. she continues to astound. love sara

sara gilfenbaum <sara@free.midcoast.com>
waldoboro, me USA - Thursday, December 16, 1999 at 06:57:14 (EST)

Philip,

   Thanks for sharing the letter and poem in this brave season of wrap, unwrap, play with, pack. Perhaps in this coming moon the daybird will sing a soft nightsong for us all. We'll remember, listen, and look.

D <dconover@compasslight.com>
USA - Friday, December 17, 1999 at 20:50:25 (EST)

Dear Philip,

   I read your poem last night and wept for her, you, the boys, for myself and my current situation…and now, this morning as I write this, I understand again that these tears are about a lot of things, but they are mostly about love..love lost, love current, and love, perhaps, to be. It's what keeps me going and the love that you and Jamie and the boys have shared with all of us has really helped me more than I can convey. What you have done (all of you at 11 Maple Street) is big and brave and important, and how can any of us thank you enough or tell you enough how deeply it is received and appreciated.
   Peter

Camden, - Saturday, December 18, 1999 at 07:55:56 (EST)

   I too visit this place from time to time, marveling at the tender love and open vulnerability I find. Thank you for sharing your journey. Once again you offer gifts even to strangers. In this dark and holy season, I am moved that

Jamie sent you her letter and by your response in poetry.
   Blessings and Love, Catharine

Catharine Scherer <JASHODA@Aol.com>
Spokane, WA USA - Monday, December 20, 1999 at 12:03:18 (EST)

   Why, after so long, do I return to this site? In part it's because my Christmasy house is suddenly quiet and I have a moment to think of friends. But there is something else that pulls…Could it be that this site begins to serve and participate in ways that women have always known, connecting across continents and generations, and even time barriers…I, too, wept at Jamie's prescience about your first Christmas without her, about the intimate thread of tradition which connects families everywhere, and your shock, the handwriting, the cold icy blast that makes this all so real.
   This was originally intended as a "personal e-mail to Philip" but when I identified so tenderly with another letter and discovered it was from Peter, I realized I should make this an open letter as well. God bless us all and the ties that bind. Love, Jeri

Jeri
Wayland, USA - Sunday, December 26, 1999 at 22:33:32 (EST)

MILLENNIAL CHRISTMAS   January 8

It must be hard, friends say,
The first Christmas
For you and the boys,
I guess, they mean,
Without mother or wife,
To do it all. But I guess
I knew, even long ago,
I could, if it came to this,
Do it all; God knows
I watched enough times
While you arrayed
Candles, calendars, and creche;
And pushed the stone up the hill
Toward that razor's edge
Where the sum of all effort
Exactly cancels all that force
You or me to our knees
While life teeters on the rim
Suspended there
In the eternal moment
Of your dying breath
Before the stone comes
Crashing down December's ridge
Into the drear light
Of another January dawn.

PWC

215

Afterwords

. . . .

*Keep your eyes open, look for her,
and try to keep her alive in you.*

Sam Conkling 3 May 2000

April 2000   Our Summer Islands   James Lane Conkling

> *"By drinking tea together, I believe we may, indeed, solve some of the greatest problems in the world."*
>
> Jamien Morehouse, March, 1986

March 6
· · · ·

Jamien's favorite teapot

Dear Friends,

Jamien ended her first Tea Ceremony letter in 1986 with a postscript. She wrote that she had bought Tim and Sam (ages four and two at the time) a tea set for Valentine's Day and that they were going to join her for tea on the first day of spring.

I'm not sure the boys remember that first tea, but ever since then the five of us here have been steeped in Jamien's urgent appeal that we reach out to connect with each other as a way of engaging the human heart in healing the wounds of this world, large and small. We propose to help re-light a passionate flame of remembrance of what is truly important in life by inviting you to an extended tea party with friends and loved ones on the first day of spring, March 20, 2000, at 4:00 p.m., EST.

We are putting out this word by print, voice, and Web. We hope the pebble we cast into our own small pond will ripple outwards into the near and far corners as a symbol of our interconnectedness. For truly, the waters of the world that we drink, that we live by, and that we one day return to are a powerful reminder of what links us all in life and death.

And this tea water also reminds us that life is both short and long and that we go on and on into our futures, and that generations echo down the long corridors of time, and that we hear a rejoicing, a high descant over the earth's lamentations.

218

As our lives move through spring's March into May, please also know that we are all well and happy. The boys are on the bows of their own strong vessels, charting their courses into their future. We are all blessed by the strong memories we have of our incandescent time together. May you be also. And may you mark your calendars for June 25th this year when the new Jamien Morehouse Wing of the Farnsworth Art Museum will open in Rockland with a huge celebration of the interconnections of islands and art; of our pasts and futures. And if you are so moved, share your stories of your lives and loves with us via postcard or posted at http://www.jamien.com.

May it ever be so, with love forever,

Philip, Tim, Sam, James, and Micah

I'd Like Her to be Proud of Me

For the past year now, the five of us in residence here at 11 Maple Street have been missing Jamien each in our own ways, each for our own reasons. The house misses her: it has truly turned into a bachelor pad and lacks organization. The five guys that Jamien mentored still struggle with tough questions that she would have had immediate answers to: what laundry detergent should we use? whose job is it to take out the compost? how do I iron a pair of pants?

I miss her. It's been a year since she died and I'm off to college. I really miss the guidance she provided – she always seemed to know the best solution to any problem. I'd like to ask her, "have I picked a good college?" "how should I prepare for leaving home?" "will you come visit me at my dorm every once in a while?"

And I'd like for her to be proud of me. I'd like to show her my acceptance letters and the grades I got in English class this year and my latest computer programming projects because I know she would be proud, and that always meant so much coming from her.

Every day I am reminded of mom and the impact she had on the world. The **jamien.com** Web site is an amazing testament to her legacy – the sheer volume of posts that have been made on the site speaks to the awesome effect that one person can have on so many others.
Thanks for everything, mom.

Tim Conkling, May 3, 2000

Keep your eyes open, Look for her

Once someone you love is gone forever, a part of your life is taken too. It's hard to understand what things will be like without someone as close as your mother, and time doesn't seem to help me comprehend our situation. I still don't sincerely believe Mom's gone, and frequently find myself meeting her in dreams, or having joyful thoughts of her showing up back on the front steps of 11 Maple Street after returning from another long trip to Russia.

I have spent a year without her now, but still, everyday I miss her even more. She is someone who will never leave my life and that is truly wonderful. The first day of spring, a day she always celebrated, reinstilled and reaffirmed her image in my mind. We took our basket of tea out to her secret rock garden in a tribute to her. Sitting around the granite boulder which served as our table top, I think I felt her presence. I wonder what she is thinking, but my guess is that she's happy. That day reminded me of something she said. Before she lost her voice, she called all her boys around her bed and told us to keep our eyes open after she died, because although she would be gone from her body, she said she would still exist in smaller things, and she hoped we would recognize them. Although these smaller things don't always jump out at me, when they come back to mind, I realize she was right…she is there. Jamien Morehouse is someone who will never leave my life, and that is truly wonderful.

Mostly where she shows her face occasionally is in people who were lucky enough, even in the remotest of ways, to come into contact with her. That is where she will never die. She stamped us all with a little piece of her extraordinary personality. She had no end of what she offered to teach. She had a selfless way of living; because of her ideals and principles, I am who I am. Keep your eyes open, look for her, and try to keep her alive in you.

Sam Conkling, May 3, 2000

In closing

Jamien Morehouse believed in miracles of the everyday sort.

She believed deeply in the interconnectedness not just of all life but of all experience.

She believed the cosmos was winking at her in merriment whenever a streetlight or headlight blinked out, which happened often as she passed by.

She believed she had lived previous lives, at least one of them on the steppes of Mongolia, among horsemen and their families, who lived in yurts and moved about the landscape.

She believed that contributing to the joyfulness of children is the greatest gift we give to the world.

She believed that many voices speak through our hands and hearts when we feverishly create art or music from tattered pieces of existence begging to be used.

She believed that islands are places not of isolation but of connections with each other and the rest of creation.

She believed we express the best of ourselves through simple rituals, like sharing tea, adventurous picnics, and evening meals.

She believed in saying grace and giving thanks.

Through the example of living these simple beliefs, she transformed the lives and experiences of nearly everyone she met. These beliefs took on greater urgency after she was diagnosed with breast cancer.

She parried cancer's thrusts with a dancer's skill and successfully battled it in close quarters, both night and day, for more than a decade. Although we consulted oncologists in Boston and natural healers throughout New England, she learned mostly to trust the instincts of her heart, which helped her learn how to listen to her own body. Most of all Jamien learned how to allow fear to visit, but not to take up residency in her body and mind.

To our great surprise, we discovered that living as if every breath, every word, and every day matters is a fine way to live, though often tiring and difficult. We learned that the spirit is found just beyond the point you think you cannot go and that it is wondrous, deep, and unending. And when her end came, as it must soon or late for us all, we felt there was truly nothing we had left unsaid or undone.

This book is a record of the correspondence, the remembrance, the transcendence that ultimately took on a life of its own, proving to all of us, believers and non-believers alike, that love never ends.

Life is so big.

Philip Conkling

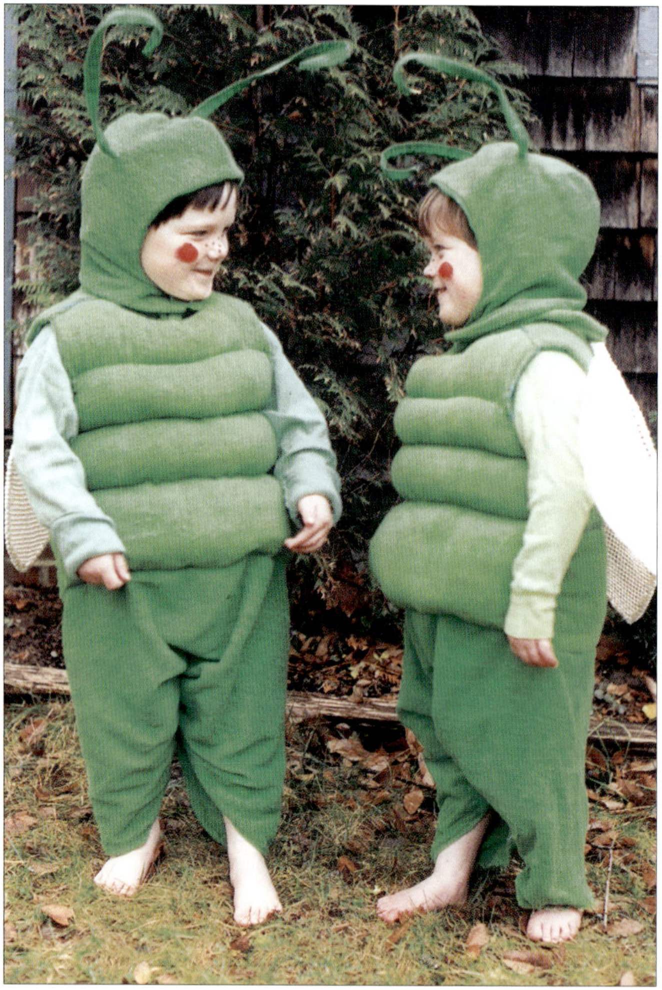

Somewhere

They say no one ever truly leaves,
They are always there, somewhere.
Maybe that's why I see my beloved mother
Almost everywhere.
Beautiful Jamien,
Darting, leaping, to and from
Every natural thing;
A wild seal that investigates
Closer than the others, "Hi, Mom."
A bird that seems to hide
But follows me, "Hi, Mom."
So maybe it's true
You are out there
Somewhere.

Micah Conkling, May 3, 2000

Acknowledgements

This book called forth a wonderful outpouring of kindnesses from many more people than can be thanked by name. To the hundreds of friends and family whose postings on the Web first inpsired the idea of this book, our family is more grateful with each passing day at the depth of your continuing love that has been shared so unselfishly. We could not reproduce each letter here, so we tried to select ones that reflect the diversity of friendships and expeiences in Jamien's life. For those whose letters are reproduced here, we thank you collectively even though we were not able in the time alotted to thank each of you individually.

To those who allowed examples of Jamien's fish, banners and other art to be reproduced here, I would like to extend special words of gratitude. Mary Amory, Tom Beuscher, Deborah Meehan and Bruce Morehouse lent their fish by Jamien; Amy Fischer, Deborah Meehan and Wendy Weiler lent their hats by Jamien; Kalla Buchholz, Wendy Harris, Bruce Morehouse, Kelly Richards and Frank Simon lent banners by Jamien. Additional heartfelt thanks are extended to Antonia Munroe whose silkscreened prayer flags for Jamien are reproduced here, and to Sara Gilfenbaum who shared her tea letters by Jamien. Important photographs wer also contributed by Karin Cole, Alison Kennedy, Dick and Lee Morehouse, Bruce Morehouse, Peter Ralston and Anita Brosius-Scott.

The production of this book could not have been accomplsihed without help from Steve and Debbie Morrison at PDQ who photographed Jamien's work. Steve Waterman and Charlie Oldham made the scans for the layout, Anne Leslie provided expert copy editing, Judy Tierney chased scores of details and David Platt coordinated the production schedule.

Finally, this book made the huge leap from wishful concept to lasting reality through the extraordinary generosity extended by Charlie and Julie Cawley to the entire extended Conkling-Morehouse family.

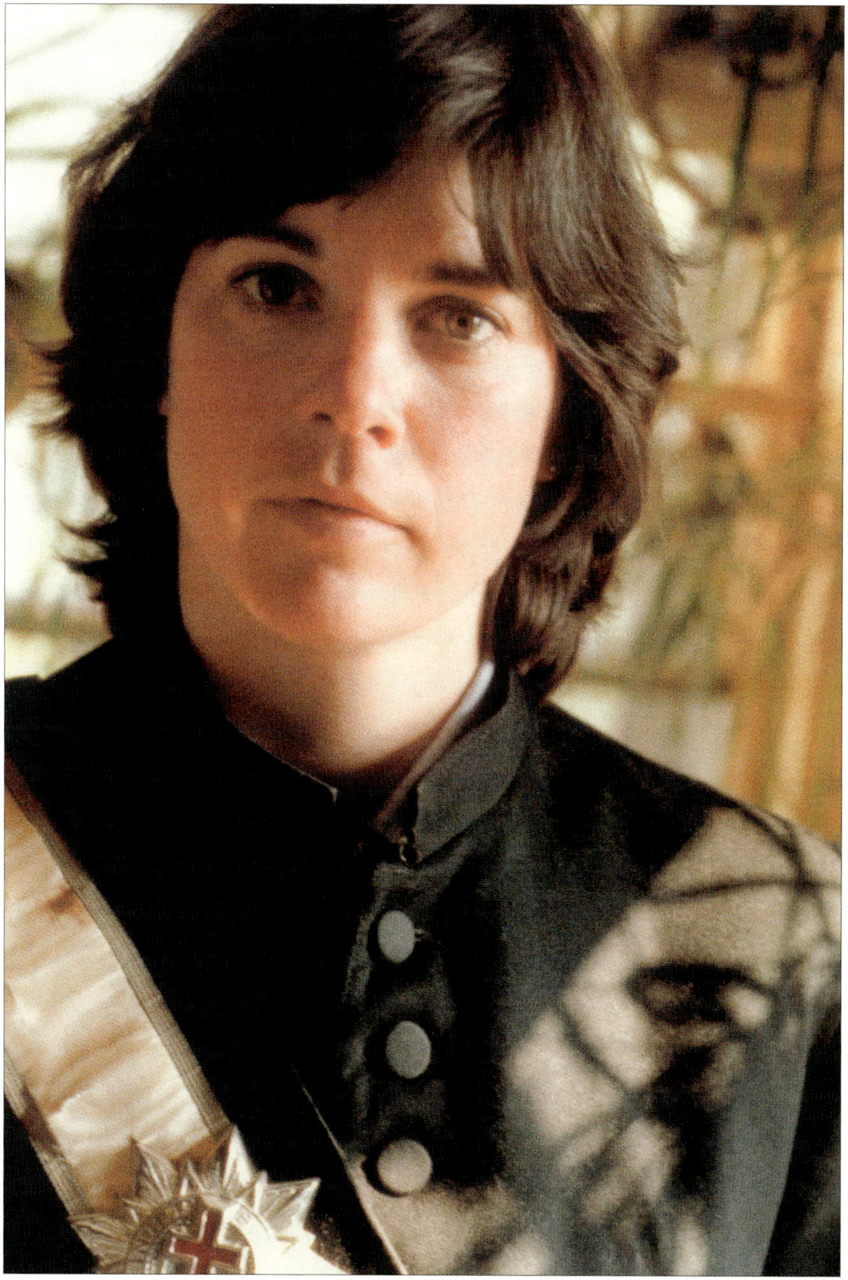